The Gospel train's a-coming, I hear it just at hand,
I hear the car wheels rumbling, and rolling through the land.
I hear the train a-coming, she's coming round the curve,
She's loosened all her steam and brakes, and straining every nerve.
The fare is cheap and all can go, the rich and poor are there,
No second class aboard this train, no difference in the fare.

Spiritual

Now we have received not the spirit of the world, but the Spirit which
is from God, that we might understand the gifts bestowed on us by God.

1 Corinthians 2:12

Do and dare what is right, not swayed by the whim of the moment.
Bravely take hold of the real, not dallying now with what might be.
Not in the flight of ideas but only in action is freedom.
Make up your mind and come out into the tempest of living.
God's command is enough and your faith in him to sustain you.
Then at last freedom will welcome your spirit amid great rejoicing.

from Bonhoeffer's "Stations on the Way to Freedom"

NO DIFFERENCE
IN THE FARE

*Dietrich Bonhoeffer
and the Problem of Racism*

Josiah Ulysses Young III

WILLIAM B. EERDMANS PUBLISHING COMPANY
GRAND RAPIDS, MICHIGAN / CAMBRIDGE, U.K.

© 1998 Wm. B. Eerdmans Publishing Co.
255 Jefferson Ave. S.E., Grand Rapids, Michigan 49503 /
P.O. Box 163, Cambridge CB3 9PU U.K.

Printed in the United States of America

03 02 01 00 99 98   7 6 5 4 3 2 1

Library of Congress Cataloging-in-Publication Data

Young, Josiah U. (Josiah Ulysses)
No difference in the fare: Dietrich Bonhoeffer and the problem of racism /
Josiah Ulysses Young III.
p.   cm.
Includes bibliographical references and index.
ISBN 0-8028-4465-0 (pbk.: alk. paper)
1. Bonhoeffer, Dietrich, 1906-1945 — Contributions in theology of race relations.
2. Race relations — Religious aspects — Christianity.
3. Racism — Religious aspects — Christianity.
4. Afro-Americans — Social conditions.
5. Racism — United States.
I. Title.
BT734.2.Y68   1998
305.8'00973 — dc21   98-28330
                                                                          CIP

To my children,

Josiah and Thandi

Contents

Foreword, by John D. Godsey   ix

Acknowledgments   xii

Abbreviations   xiv

Preface   1

Introduction   13

1. "Lord Help the Poor and Needy":
   Rereading Bethge's *Dietrich Bonhoeffer*   21

2. Old Time Religion: Rereading
   The Communion of Saints and *Act and Being* —
   Bonhoeffer's Early Theology   50

3. Poor Pilgrims of Sorrow:
   African-Americans and Dietrich Bonhoeffer   87

4. "I'm Going to Lay Down This Heavy Load":
   Bonhoeffer's Costly Grace   125

5. "There's Room for Many a More":
   Bonhoeffer's Legacy for the Twenty-first Century   159

Bibliography   172

Index of Names   177

Foreword

Yet another book about Dietrich Bonhoeffer? Yes! This one breaks new ground by demonstrating the pertinence of the martyred German theologian's thought for analyzing and addressing North America's most intractable social problem: racism. Bonhoeffer's biblically based opposition to Nazi anti-Semitism, which led to his imprisonment and execution by the Gestapo over fifty years ago, has been explored by many writers. But it took an African-American theologian of the stature of Josiah Young to reveal the way Bonhoeffer's understanding of Christian faith provides an antidote to the mistaken and cruel notion of white supremacy that has caused inordinate suffering among black Americans from the days of slavery until now.

Josiah Ulysses Young III, Professor of Systematic Theology at Wesley Theological Seminary in Washington, D.C., is well equipped to write *No Difference in the Fare: Dietrich Bonhoeffer and the Problem of Racism.* A native of New York City who was educated at Morehouse College in Atlanta and Union Theological Seminary in New York, Young became interested in Bonhoeffer and liberation theologies early in his career. His doctoral dissertation and first book, *Black and African Theologies: Siblings or Distant Cousins?* (Orbis Books, 1986), probed various Afro-American and African theologies in his own "long search for wholeness and identity." This was followed by *A Pan-African Theology: Providence and the Legacies of the Ancestors* (Africa World Press, 1992), in which he explored "the redemptive, Pan-African implications of the African heritage," which he contrasted with "the terror of Eurocentric praxes of domination."

In Bonhoeffer, who himself had pursued postdoctoral studies at Union in 1930-31 and, more important, had spent most of his spare time that year in youth ministry at the Abyssinian Baptist Church in Harlem, Young encountered a kindred spirit whose theology was utterly opposed to racist attitudes and practices. Already in his first two writings, *Sanctorum Communio* and *Act and Being,* Bonhoeffer had developed an understanding of the interrelationship between God, self, and others that assured the freedom, dignity, and "strangeness" of "the other" in the "I-Thou relationship." The fact that the "alien Thou" is willed by God and is to be loved as such destroys the basis of racism, whose law is "Thou shalt love only the Same."

Early in his sojourn in the United States, Bonhoeffer became aware of the "race problem" not only in society but, to his consternation, in the churches as well. Because of a false theory of racial superiority, many white Americans, he found, denigrated their black brothers and sisters rather than recognizing and rejoicing in their created differences. Instead of following Jesus Christ in "being there for others," white racists cultivated a life of "being against others," namely, those whose skin pigmentation was different from their own. Bonhoeffer's American experience turned out to be prologue to his experience of Hitler's vicious racist attacks against the Jews that occurred soon after his return to Germany.

What Josiah Young has done in this remarkable book is to examine the main theological writings of Bonhoeffer, from those early dissertations to his letters and papers from prison, in order to show how Bonhoeffer's thought, at its core and at every stage, is inimical to racist views and promotes a just and loving way of life-in-community that embraces diverse groups of people, particularly those who have been downtrodden and scorned. With the help of Bonhoeffer's acute insights, the author exposes the evil of white racism in America during the past four hundred years and also suggests ways of moving from divisive bigotry to inclusive community. To aid in his effort to highlight the effects of racism and to show how the African heritage actually supports the nonracist views of a Christianity true to the gospel of Christ, Young cites a number of African-American and African writers throughout his work: W. E. B. Du Bois, James Weldon Johnson, Toni Morrison, Cornel West, B. Adoukonou, F. Eboussi-Boulaga, and many others. He also demonstrates his familiarity with the spirituals by frequently using them to drive home his point.

This volume combines sound scholarship, depth of insight, and lucid prose. It illumines a horrible human problem found not just in North America or in Nazi Germany but in many parts of the world. It enlivens and broadens Bonhoeffer studies. It helps us understand Martin Luther's dictum: "But this is the Christian faith: to know what you should do and what has been given to you." Above all, its purpose is to promote the kind of concrete action that will overcome racism in all its forms and lead to a more just and caring society. Readers from all walks of life will profit from the wisdom of Josiah Young.

John D. Godsey

Acknowledgments

Right off the bat, I must thank John Godsey, a colleague and a friend: Thanks, John, for the seal of approval — the gracious Foreword — and for being a fellow-sufferer for the sake of racial justice.

Another friend and colleague, Douglas Meeks, has also backed this project: Thanks, Doug, for your support — for your belief in this venture even before I sat down during my sabbatical to pull it out of thin air. I am grateful as well to Bobby McClain, yet another colleague and friend: Thank you, Bob, for believing in this project and for your witness to the evils of racism. Thanks are also due to James Cone. His unqualified approval of this work encouraged me to seek its publication.

I have benefited greatly from the critical, supportive readings by Larry Rasmussen and Christopher Morse. I thank them both for the time they took to read my work and for their constructive suggestions.

Words cannot express my gratitude to Mr. William B. Eerdmans. I take my hat off to him for deciding to publish *No Difference in the Fare,* for believing, indeed, that "the fare is cheap and all can go"!

Pamela Monroe, my wife and truest friend, read the manuscript and improved it greatly with her editor's eye. How great it is to have a live-in editor! *Thanks for keeping me in line and putting up with my foolishness.*

Acknowledgments

My son, Josiah Monroe Young, whom we call Joey, is quite proud of the fact that his father writes books. "So, Dad," he said to me on a number of occasions, "when is your Bonhoeffer book coming out?" "Well, son, I don't know if it is ever coming out." "Aw, come on, Dad, you *know* it is." Well, thanks, son, for your faith in me. And to my baby girl, Thandi — her name means "the Beloved-one" — thanks for reminding me each time I look on your angel-face what hope is all about. May you and your brother be judged by the content of your characters — gifts to the world that you are.

Abbreviations

AB	*Act and Being*
CF	*Creation and Fall*
COD	*Cost of Discipleship*
CTC	*Christ the Center*
E	*Ethics*
LPP	*Letters and Papers from Prison*
LT	*Life Together*
NRS	*No Rusty Swords*
SC	*The Communion of Saints*

Preface

Many years ago, two pastors piqued my interest in Dietrich Bonhoeffer. I had come to know them as I worked as an assistant pastor in upstate New York. First cousins to each other, they were assistant ministers in a Pentecostal church, the Sanctified Church; and their church was one of the holyroller churches that made up the Soul Saving Station — a constellation of Pentecostal churches. One might have thought that these pastors would have been far removed from Bonhoeffer — the world-class, highly privileged, highly accomplished German theologian. But as African-Americans, they were overwhelmed by racial injustice. Desperate to understand it, they looked to Bonhoeffer for theological insight, even though much about him appears to have been chauvinistic.

There are, after all, a number of reasons why Bonhoeffer would not seem the obvious choice for a champion of racial justice. Thomas Day, for instance, contends that Bonhoeffer was a bit sexist (look, for example, at Bonhoeffer's "A Wedding Sermon from a Prison Cell"). Thinking Bonhoeffer an elitist, Day also questions the correctness of Bonhoeffer's judgment that the French Revolution was at the root of the Nazi rabble: "Anti-democrat Bonhoeffer," writes Day, "saw the chaos of his age as resulting from the loss of belief in the divine right of social structures"; and it was that theologically

1

based position that accounted for Bonhoeffer's sense of "the continuum he saw between the democratic idealism of the French revolution and the nihilism of the Nazis" (Day 1975, 372). So tied to paternalistic authority is Day's "anti-democrat" Bonhoeffer that he agreed that a "military-based monarchy" would suit Germany's immediate needs, if Hitler were toppled (Day 1975). Bonhoeffer's view on the superior and the inferior, which he linked in his *Ethics* to the master and the servant, tends to reinforce Day's impression that Bonhoeffer was an elitist. Indeed, Bonhoeffer's view as to why the New Testament is soft on slavery, as found in that same book, *Ethics,* might well make an African-American think Bonhoeffer had made common cause with the master.

Bonhoeffer's elitist views — he once complained that psychoanalytical approaches to ministry were so voyeuristic as to be "far too unaristocratic for the Word of God to ally itself with them" — suggest that he was worlds apart from the black pastors who claimed him. They were unaristocratic themselves: not even bourgeois, they were a generation removed from sharecroppers and unskilled laborers. The disabilities of slavery were all too evidently about them. Bonhoeffer, on the other hand, was groomed in a household where both parents were of a long line of the well-to-do. His father, the son of the President of the High Court at Tübingen, was a prominent professor and highly thought-of psychiatrist — an accomplished man descended from goldsmiths, clergymen, doctors, councillors and burgomasters. Bonhoeffer's mother, who herself educated her highly accomplished children early on, was the daughter of a distinguished theologian, as well as the granddaughter of an even more celebrated theological scholar.

Appealing to an uncompleted play Bonhoeffer penned in 1943, which involves dialogue between the bourgeois Christophe and the proletarian Henri, André Dumas argues that Bonhoeffer never disowned his bourgeois ballasts — his moorings in Berlin's upper crust. Despite the fact that Bonhoeffer's line emerged from *les nouveaux riches,* and not the landed gentry, Dumas argues that Bonhoeffer's work has an aristocratic nuance — *un accent "aristocra-*

tique," he calls it — one reminiscent of Simone Weil's sense of security. (Weil asserts that security is indispensable for the soul — that no one should have to suffer great angst due to unemployment, systemic repression, and so forth.) Only the well-heeled, and Bonhoeffer was surely among them, can usually afford such security (Dumas 1968, 47). Bonhoeffer's proletarian Henri reminded him of this: that Bonhoeffer had taken much for granted — namely this *sécurité,* solid ground beneath his feet, a good measure of which stayed beneath him even while in prison.

Arrested initially for improprieties having to do with protocol within the *Abwehr,* the German military intelligence department, the well-connected, but incarcerated, Bonhoeffer was still close to middle-class amenities. After twelve days in a cold and clammy cell, with bed covers so putrid he could not bear to use them, he was given certain privileges. (His cousin was the City Commandant of Berlin, with jurisdiction over the military prisons.) In fact, Bonhoeffer enjoyed a bit of clout while in prison. At one point, he could, and did, make life difficult for a person he disliked: a fellow whose anti-Semitism offended the Aryan Bonhoeffer (see chapter five). Bonhoeffer was torn over these prison amenities. "While this was a great relief to me personally," he wrote, "it was most embarrassing to see how everything changed from that moment."

> I was put into a more spacious cell, which one of the men cleaned everyday for me; I was offered larger rations, which I always refused, as they would have been at the expense of the other prisoners; the captain fetched me for a daily walk, with the result that the staff treated me with studied politeness — in fact, several of them came to apologize: "We didn't know," etc. It was painful.

With the exception of the period just before the very end, Bonhoeffer's prison stint was less brutal than those justice-seekers suffer today in repressive regimes.

Still another factor contradicts the idea that Bonhoeffer was a comrade of the oppressed. Ernst Feil writes that Bonhoeffer's idiom,

3

"world come of age," meant, in part, that a great adulthood has sprung from modernity. Liberated from medieval provincialism, and taking metaphysics as well as religion to task, this new world was not all that bad: As Bonhoeffer saw it, aspersions cast on this grownup world were meaningless, inglorious, and "unChristian." And I can see his point — not a single one of us can go back to a time free of the crises of today. Who questions the fact that modernity, meaning "the adulthood of the world," is here to stay? To the extent, in addition, that such an adulthood divests us of the illusion of a pristine yesterday — an illusion that flees from the real world — who can advocate a turning back of the clock?

But at whose expense does one say (as Bonhoeffer said), "Man has learnt to deal with himself in all questions of importance without recourse to the 'working hypothesis' called 'God'"? To whom does this really apply: "In questions of science, art, and ethics this has become an understood thing at which one now hardly dares to tilt" (LPP, 325)? Okay. But to what extent have these things, this science, and that art, as well as these ethics, taken us into consideration — we victims of racism, we heirs to the tragic aftermaths of slavery or colonization, we still behind the eight ball? Would it not also be Christian to consider our voices when one evaluates whether the discussion of yesterday — meaning whatever life was like before westernization (which is the upshot of this grownup world for much of the Third World) — is "pointless," "ignoble," and "unChristian"? It is not at all clear that we are *all* so indebted to the Enlightenment.

Yet all these things — Bonhoeffer's chauvinism, privilege, and his Eurocentric perspective — do not in themselves discount his work in my book. Neither would the revelation that he was not quite as taken with blacks as one might think. *No Difference in the Fare* draws much of its substance from Bonhoeffer's encounter with African-Americans. But that encounter by itself does not say a whole lot. He wrote nothing lengthy about us; only bits and pieces here and there — such as, "People say in America that the Negroes survived because they had not forgotten how to laugh, whereas the Indians went under because they were too 'proud'" (LPP, 224). (His

4

point being that there was a virtue in black humor akin to the promising spirit of Germany's younger generation.)

It could very well be that Bonhoeffer was attracted to blacks only insofar as they bore the impress of the West. The Africanness so critical for a comprehensive appreciation of our blackness — which is a point I will argue later — was likely as Eurocentrically construed by Bonhoeffer as was his well-intentioned challenge to the 1934 Fanö conference — "Are we to be put to shame by heathens in the East" (Bethge 1985, 331). (Bonhoeffer was referring to Gandhi.) Aside from a few insightful references to Africa — which I find to be very significant — Bonhoeffer was a bit negative about the continent. When a teenager, he visited North Africa and had a somewhat harrowing experience: "One should not spend a longer time in Africa without preparation," he wrote in his diary. "The shock is too great, and increases from day to day, so that one is glad to return to Europe again" (Bethge 1985, 38).

I wonder too whether Bonhoeffer had blacks in mind when he wrote from prison to his best friend and "soul brother," Eberhard Bethge, about the paranoia of "outcasts" and "pariahs":

> Just as the vulgar mind isn't satisfied till it has seen some highly placed personage "in his bath," or in other embarrassing situations, so it is here. There is a kind of evil satisfaction in knowing that everyone has his failings and weak spots. *In my contacts with the "outcasts" of society, its "pariahs," I've noticed repeatedly that mistrust is the dominant motive in their judgement of other people. Every action, even the most unselfish, of a person of high repute is suspected from the outset.* (LPP, 344-45, emphasis added)

Perhaps Bonhoeffer's statement was to make the point that the all-too-religious penchant for sniffing out a person's Achilles heel — "the range of his intimate life, from prayer to his sexual life" — is but a form of "religious blackmail" (344). None but the vulgar-minded, outcasts, and pariahs, so to speak, would stoop so low as to invade the privacy of persons in order to hit them where it hurts.

On the other hand, it is clear that in his disdain for the Nazis, Bonhoeffer thought they had displaced order with disorder — "a revolution from below, a revolt of inferiority" — which gave license, in fact, to this profane religiousness that typified a reigning, collective attitude. Is Bonhoeffer, then, drawing some analogy between wary African-Americans and the Nazis's holier-than-Thou game? If so, it is not so much to insult blacks as to put down the Nazis. For his assertion — "These 'outcasts' are to be found in all grades of society. In a flower-garden they grub around only for the dung on which the flowers grow" — would certainly apply to the Nazis (345).

But if there is such an analogy being drawn here — in which Bonhoeffer's encounter with blacks is used as a foil to denounce the Nazis — it is a poor one: Blacks are hardly merely outcasts or pariahs; and they have good reason to be paranoid about the motives of the Other. Given the insights one finds in Bonhoeffer's early theology, and given the witness of his own life, he surely knew that.

So perhaps Bonhoeffer did not have blacks in mind when he wrote what he did. And even though Bonhoeffer failed to mention Africa at least a couple of times when he considered Asia — which is a significant omission for one so committed to the *world* — I still find that persons committed to racial justice, and aware of the significance of African-Americans' struggle, can discover, in Bonhoeffer's life and thought, useful theological insights that strengthen one in the struggle against racism.

The young ministers who taught me about Bonhoeffer surely thought so. As African-Americans, desperate to understand the racial injustice which surrounded them, they looked to Bonhoeffer for theological insight. They had studied him while they were in seminary and felt he had lived out the meaning of the gospel — a meaning akin to the reason their congregation danced and shouted in church every Sunday and several days during the rest of the week.

In the height of worship, their flock appeared to know that rotten luck was not a misfortune God had ordained. They were black, and because they were, they were poor and barely schooled. (Not that

6

all black people are poor, and all whites well off and literate. Still, poverty and blackness go together in a way that must be admitted if any one of us is to deal honestly and squarely with the problem of racism. To be black in the United States, as well as in the world, is a serious disability.) But what made the folks happy in the Soul Saving Station was their faith that *God* bore them no enmity. They had placed their hope in a just Providence, *leaning on the Lord*.

If one takes Bonhoeffer to heart, the faith that moved the folk to shout preceded their joyous abandon. They were enjoying what had been given them — it was theirs, but (then again) not theirs. Without detracting from the fact that one who gives a gift means for the recipient to have it, we miss the character of the gift itself if we fail to see that the giving of it is the essential thing. That it is more blessed to give than to receive is no empty platitude; and this blessedness is the gift of the giver, not the receiver.

A true gift has no rhyme or reason. Freely given, it always takes us by surprise: We cannot figure out why we have been so gifted, for a gift's whence rests in the enigma of the genuinely gracious giver — the truly disinterested lover. Who in today's world, racked by love's antithesis, can figure out, really, the unsolicited call of such love? How much more of a mystery (always an important word for Bonhoeffer) would giftedness be if *God* were the Giver.

Faith, for Bonhoeffer, is precisely that: God's Gift. And if faith is just such a gift, then when, as well as how, the shouting congregation received their faith was hidden from them. The givenness of their faith (one might well call this the "heavenliness" of their faith) — which would be God's very own province — was not accessible to them. Not even in the height of worship. Whether their highly stylized expressions were faithful depended entirely upon "the mystery of predestination" — upon whether some of them had truly, and once upon a time, looked to (or looked on) the ultimate side of reality. To use the language of Bonhoeffer's *Ethics,* their highly energized worship belonged to the penultimate; so what mattered was not the captivating richness of their charisma. If Bonhoeffer has credibility, all that mattered was that their faith was bestowed by God — a givenness expressed in the classic Protestant idiom "justification by grace and faith alone."

I got the sense that those shouting and dancing people really believed, though the congregation was far from perfect: charges of adultery against the senior pastor, the making of sanctified behavior into a bogus legalism, the backbiting and petty power struggles to which most churches are prey. But those flaws aside, the folk appeared committed, with the totality of their emotional and physical selves, to their God. Without breaking tried and true tradition, they expressed their faith with startling conviction.

Bonhoeffer was no stranger to such goings-on. When a very young man, he spent time in Harlem, New York City, which is but a few blocks from Union Theological Seminary, where he studied. Eberhard Bethge, Bonhoeffer's principal biographer, writes that Bonhoeffer was a sought-after speaker in 1930-1931, the year he visited America, but "avoided indiscriminately *squandering* himself. . . . He allowed himself to become really involved only in the Negro district of Harlem" (Bethge 1985, 109, emphasis added).

Making Bethge's point, André Dumas asserts that Bonhoeffer could not get enough of Harlem. (*Il visite assidûment Harlem.*) And he witnessed there what he called the unrivalled, "widespread" vigor of black revival preaching. (The African-American scholar W. E. B. Du Bois has characterized such vigor as the Frenzy of black churches, in which blacks have retained the ways of their enslaved forbearers, who learned the excited behavior from their African ancestors.) Within the contexts of such charismatic gatherings, Bonhoeffer thought "the Gospel of Jesus Christ, the savior of the sinner, is really preached and accepted with great welcome and visible emotion" (NRS, 109).

I wager that Bonhoeffer's ongoing commitment to obey Christ concretely — which landed him in prison, in fact — was related to the "visible emotion" of the black worship that he experienced. The very visible demonstration that the Holy Ghost was in the church may have revealed more about Bonhoeffer's faith than his ethics did.

Could it be that something about that emotion gets to the heart of Bonhoeffer's appropriation of the Protestant idiom, *actus directus*? This idiom, about which I will say more in chapter two, is integral to his *Act and Being,* but let me say something about it now.

Related to the *fides directa* of "Protestant dogmatics" (which directs us to the Giver of faith, who is the Other responsible for faith's mysteriousness), *actus directus,* as I see it, has three implications.

First, there is Bonhoeffer's sense that one is so directed to Christ that one can look nowhere else — surely not to oneself, nor to anyone else. "He sees only Christ, as his Lord and his God" (AB, 181). That seeing of Christ alone brings to mind, second, a spiritual often sung in the black church, "Woke Up This Morning." "Oh, I woke up this morning with my mind . . . stayed on Jesus" is the leading line of that spiritual, and it brings to mind as well the way a people "get the Spirit" — to such an extent that they lose themselves in an altered state, for they experience the Holy head on. James Baldwin's *Go Tell It on the Mountain* vividly brings this to light. In Baldwin's novel, a young black boy, also a member of the Sanctified Church — who (if you will suspend disbelief) lives in Harlem around the time Bonhoeffer was there — is laid flat by the power of the Holy Ghost:

> Then John *saw* the Lord — for a moment only; and the darkness, for a moment only, was filled with a light he could not bear. Then, in a moment, he was set *free*; his tears sprang as from a fountain; his heart, like a fountain of waters, burst. Then he cried: "Oh blessed Jesus! Oh, Lord Jesus! Take me through." (Baldwin 1952, 204, emphases added)

One is struck by Bonhoeffer's sense of the *actus directus* because John is stayed on Christ: *Oh Lord Jesus! Take me through!*

Third, I find that Bonhoeffer's *actus directus* bears an affinity to the "inward eye," an idiom from *The Bluest Eye* — a novel by the Pulitzer Prize- and Nobel Prize-winning writer Toni Morrison. She uses the inward eye in conjunction with the "bluest eye," which symbolizes the power of a reigning and unjust aesthetic:

> Love is never any better than the lover. Wicked people love wickedly, violent people love violently, weak people love weakly, stupid people love stupidly. . . . There is no gift for the beloved. The lover alone possesses his gift of love. The loved one is shorn, neutralized, frozen in the glare of the lover's inward eye. (Morrison, 1972, 159-60)

Morrison's novel is an indictment of the one who "loves" stupidly, wickedly, violently, weakly, thereby snaring the "beloved" in the iciness of the tyrannical self. But one's inward eye might well oppose such tyranny. One can also love wisely, righteously, lovingly, powerfully, thereby freeing the beloved from an impossible demand.

Symbolizing the disposition of one's heart, the character of one's love, this inward eye tells on you. What will you die for; for the sake of the bluest eye, as the Nazis did? Or, will you die in resistance to such bigotry, as blue-eyed Bonhoeffer did? Perhaps Bonhoeffer's enduring witness is this: An inward eye directed to Christ — an "I" *stayed on Jesus* — overcomes the horror of the illusion of racial hierarchy. "Can't hate your neighbor in your mind, if you keep it stayed on Jesus," the spiritual says. In the Sanctified Church, the Soul Saving Station, where I first learned about Bonhoeffer, the horror racism bred — a gravelike despair akin to Luther's *Anfechtungen* — was overcome in the dark saints' ebullient, collective witness to the One who rose from a horror not unlike theirs; as if the inward eye of the congregation were stayed on Jesus, as if the church were a collective person: *Oh blessed Jesus! Oh, Lord Jesus! Take me through.*

My suggestion, then, to reiterate, is that Bonhoeffer's interest in ethics — which involved the cultivation of relationships that rendered ethics unnecessary — was akin to that ebullient experience, both in the Soul Saving Station and in the black worship that Bonhoeffer himself experienced. In both, what saps life of joy was overcome. I bet those black folk, carrying the memory of their Afri-

10

can ancestors, had, in fact, experienced something close to what Bonhoeffer meant by the *actus directus.*

Their way of "having church" was very much different from my parish's — an aging, rapidly diminishing, white United Methodist congregation. (That church — I say this now through hindsight — could have gone far had it understood Bonhoeffer's argument that "the solution to the Negro problem is one of the decisive future tasks of the white churches" [NRS, 109]. Bonhoeffer could not accept those churches' racism toward blacks.) A United Methodist myself, I had been hired as the assistant pastor to "integrate" the church. I was to help bring the black folk into the waning congregation, thereby securing the parish's future: African-Americans would maintain the church as the old whites — who had fled the now all-black community that surrounded the church — passed away.

To make an allusion to Bonhoeffer's *The Communion of Saints,* the African-Americans — who had come to Newburgh as migrant workers — were to overcome the congregation's self-enclosed "I" with the introduction of the black "Thou." As Bonhoeffer would have it, my church was to become a Christian community, in which the law of racism, Thou shalt love only the Same, would be overcome through reveling in the difference of white and black — "I and Thou." Such difference was to be no longer a strain, but a gift, a revelation of God's love, "of God's heart, so that the Thou is to the I no longer law but gospel, and hence an object of love" (SC, 119).

My tenure at that church, however, was nearly always an occasion for insult and humiliation. One such occasion looms above all others. I recount it now because, while extreme and atypical in its candor, it goes to the heart of that syndrome that has moved me to write this book. Two white parishioners, a married pair, and the congregation's wealthiest, invited me and my wife to dinner. At the table, the wife informed us that she had been adopted and had, at first, turned down her husband's proposal of marriage. Her past was an enigma: She said to us — without batting *an eye* — that she thought she might have been "colored" and have given birth to a black baby. On the heels of this confession came another revelation of the tyrannical "I." A relative had been injured in a car accident and needed a blood transfusion. Her options were the blood of a white man with syphilis, or that of a black man without the dreaded disease. Our host made it clear that the right decision was made in rejecting the "black" blood.

I did not take her insults personally, for to do so would have been to succumb to a bitter frustration, one toxic enough to make an individual lose his "religion." After all, she did not, to make an allusion to Ralph Ellison's *Invisible Man,* see *me.* But *I* learned important lessons from what she represented. I learned to appreciate the nuances of Bonhoeffer's distinction between "faith and religion" — between the spirit-filled "Thou" of the Sanctified Church and the apotheosized "I" on the other side of the railroad tracks. For the bigotry that assailed us was not one individual's self-adoration alone; the woman's unfortunate views exposed my church's dilemma and the dilemmas of Christians I have known.

Too often Christians of different ethnic groups (and who is not ethnic?) insult one another similar to the way in which my wife and I were insulted so many years ago. The insults are unnecessary; no matter how "benign," the insults are lethal. Each is potentially the proverbial straw on the camel's back. Before you know it, someone has stepped over the line, and benignancy shows its affinity to atrocities such as the Middle Passage, the Holocaust, and all too recently, Bosnia, as well as Rwanda.

No matter how small, each encounter is tragic and illustrates what Bonhoeffer has noted for posterity. "The other person is the limit placed upon me by God. I love this limit and I shall not transgress it because of my love. . . . This means one thing is certain, that where love towards the other is destroyed [one] can only hate his limit. Then he only wants to possess or deny the other person without limit" (CF, 61). Given my African-American reading of him — this book is a rereading really — Bonhoeffer has much to offer those of us who are bothered incessantly by the sinful transgression of limits.

Introduction

Rarely do those who write on Bonhoeffer have much to say about what his legacy means in terms of racial injustice. John de Gruchy's *Bonhoeffer and South Africa* is an exception: "In the South African context the experience of blacks and the testimony of black Christians can lead — and in some instances has led — to the freedom of whites from their bondage and to the discovery of that true liberation that is to be found in Jesus Christ" (de Gruchy 1984, 75). De Gruchy has Bonhoeffer to thank for that insight. Another exception is *Bonhoeffer's Ethics: Old Europe and New Frontiers,* with an essay by the black South African Alan Boesak and other essays focusing on Bonhoeffer and India. Those essays indicate that Bonhoeffer's legacy is too valuable to be Europe's province alone.

But just look in the indices of most Bonhoeffer books: You will find few, if any, references to the fact that Bonhoeffer, during his first trip to the United States, spent much of his time in Harlem. Few make much of the fact that Bonhoeffer got to know Harlem's blacks and became good friends with a black man from Alabama, Frank Fisher. One of Bonhoeffer's classmates at Union Theological Seminary, Fisher was the one who introduced Bonhoeffer to Harlem and served as his conversation partner about the abuse of black people in America. This overlooking of an essential dimension of

13

Bonhoeffer's life suggests that all too few have considered what appears to be a necessary dimension of his life and thought: *Bonhoeffer's witness is a denunciation of the racism that threatens to sabotage the possibilities for life together in the next century*.

That raises a question: Why give only lip service to Bonhoeffer's love of Negro spirituals, to his unusualness in wanting to study with Gandhi, to his diehard resistance to Aryan-ism (meaning nazism)? Why not investigate what all of these mean in making them the angle of vision in Bonhoeffer scholarship?

To the extent that they have a bearing on the problem of racism, they are the angle of vision here. What I attempt in this book is just such a rereading of Bonhoeffer's life and thought — as reflected in Eberhard Bethge's standard Bonhoeffer biography and in Bonhoeffer's writings. The one secondary source that has engaged me more than others I have read is André Dumas's *Une théologie de la réalité: Dietrich Bonhoeffer*. I like Dumas's accent on reality: Bonhoeffer, he argues, takes us to the heart — and thus to the truth — of what is at stake in a Christian's life of faith. And what is at stake is whether we can live in this world, without illusion, and with a no-holds-barred commitment to one another — for Christ's sake!

And, once more, the illusion that strikes me as most pertinent to Bonhoeffer's legacy is that of racism. For if we have one God, then we have but one race too. One people: Pigment, as well as occiput, as well as bone, as well as writing and the steam engine are not so important as to throw one people away in favor of another. For *whose* God sanctions the racism that maims and then kills? Only the Figment of the racists' imaginations; surely not the God of all — the God of peace, Bonhoeffer's God of love. If his God is the really real, so to speak, racism must be reality's antithesis. If, as Dumas puts it, *"La théologie de Bonhoeffer est une théologie de la réalité"* — if "Bonhoeffer's theology is a theology of reality" — then it is also a worldly theology that takes racists to task.

I do not attempt a study of Bonhoeffer along the lines of John Godsey's *The Theology of Dietrich Bonhoeffer*, the book which first made Bonhoeffer's thought available to the English-speaking world.

Neither do I attempt a study after the fashion of Ernst Feil's work. Also entitled *The Theology of Dietrich Bonhoeffer,* Feil's *Bonhoeffer* seeks to lay bare "what Bonhoeffer really had in mind," particularly in regard to "Bonhoeffer's view of Christian faith lived in a religionless world" (Feil 1985, xv). I only argue that the scope of Bonhoeffer's translated theology — as it pertains to community in particular — is extended if seen in relation to the problem of racism.

I do not mean that his *The Communion of Saints* and *Act and Being* (on which I focus in Chapter 2) addressed the problem specifically. Neither, for that matter, did *The Cost of Discipleship* or *Ethics* (which I look at in Chapter 4). But how can one miss their implications for racist-free living? By virtue of the very fact that Bonhoeffer's theology is still so sound, the denunciation of racism is there, in those works, in connotation. How much more so is this the case when one reflects, seriously, on Bonhoeffer's life (the focus of Chapter 1). One sees this clearly in terms of Bonhoeffer's association with African-Americans — the focus of Chapter 3: Bonhoeffer tried to embrace, rather than to totalize, in the sense of reject, otherness — alterity.

Alterity, i.e., *altérité* — the word's significance was brought home to me by two African scholars: the theologian Barthélemy Adoukonou, and the philosopher V. Y. Mudimbe. For both, alterity involves the distinction between sameness and otherness — sameness having to do with one so-called race; otherness, with another "race." To what extent is otherness a projection of the Same? To what extent is the claim that the Negroid type is inferior to the Nordic type an ideology — a metaphysics, a religion, to use Bonhoeffer's language — with no grounding in the really real? To what extent is such an illusion yet with us, threatening more holocausts? And all because we believe, however tacitly, what Thomas Jefferson said, all too explicitly, some two centuries ago. Jefferson thought blacks and whites were so different that one would wipe out the other. He made it plain that the victims of genocide would likely be the blacks.

"The first difference that strikes us is that of color," wrote Jefferson; he wanted to know what made a people black. Does "the black of the negro [reside] in the reticular membrane between the skin and scarf-skin, or in the scarf-skin itself; [does] it proceed from the color of the blood, the color of the bile, or from that of some other secretion." Whatever the reason, Jefferson thought "the difference is fixed in nature, and is as real as if its seat and cause were better known to us. And is this difference of no importance?" It was clearly significant to him.

Whites were more aesthetically pleasing to Jefferson than blacks. Whites blush; blacks stay swarthy — "Are not the fine mixtures of red and white, the expressions of every passion by greater or less suffusions of color in the one, preferable to that eternal monotony, which reigns in the countenances, that immovable veil of black which covers the emotions of the other race? Add to these, flowing hair, a more elegant symmetry of form, their own judgment in favor of the whites, declared by their preference of them, as uniformly as is the preference of the Oranootan for the black woman over those of his own species" (Jefferson 1969, 163).

That Jefferson's is no bygone metaphysics is worrisome; it is no digression from Bonhoeffer. For the inferences to alterity in Bonhoeffer's work are light years from the alterity that holds, "The first difference which strikes us is that of color." Given his exposure to African-Americans, Bonhoeffer knew such racism had little to do with reality. Reality is born from the mix of cultures, the variance of experiences — to say nothing of the complexities of individuals, who are indispensable to the I-Thou relationships on which community is based. As Bonhoeffer makes clear in his *The Communion of Saints,* Christian community is nonexistent without alterity. To forfeit community in order to make of one phenotype a master race is an affront to Bonhoeffer's God, whose very own otherness forbids the kind of ethic that orders existence racist-ly.

Bonhoeffer knew the dangers of a racist alterity a Christian is bound to reject. "For," to quote him somewhat heuristically in terms of his *Creation and Fall,* "where thinking directs itself upon itself as the original reality it sets itself up as an object, as an object of itself,

16

and therefore it withdraws behind this object again and again — or rather, thinking is antecedent to the object it sets up" (CF, 14). That alterity is the labyrinth, the vicious circle, of the Same — the tangle of one's own, narrow self, however self-aggrandized it may be. In reality, that color-struck alterity — *The first difference which strikes us is that of color* — is alienation, self-estrangement. The alterity Bonhoeffer discusses — in his *The Communion of Saints* particularly — looks to the Other, genuinely and truly, and is not forfeited by the I, who would distort himself in caricaturing the Other. In Bonhoeffer's theology, alterity is theological and involves the dynamism of reconciliation — a point he makes in *Act and Being*.

He has it that our theologies never quite render the reality of God's otherness, though God is eminently accessible to us in Jesus Christ. Jesus is God, and yet, not God. God cannot be severed from him. God is in Christ, concretely and without precedent; but the human and divine natures in the God-man Jesus Christ are not confused. Here, absence is presence, not illusion: God's presence is "known" in a way totally dependent upon the ineffable way faith is *given*. The seeing, the actual seeing, of Jesus is never definable in a theology that is simply a reflection on the gift of Christ. Those who would divest themselves of this mystery, holding instead to a metaphysics that would measure the world God alone can measure, would, in the words of André Dumas, no longer encounter the alterity of the being of God *(rencontre l'altérité de l'être de Dieu)* (Dumas 1968, 113).

Barthélemy Adoukonou, specifically in his *Jalons pour une théologie africaine: Essai d'une herméneutique chrétienne du Vodun dahoméen,* makes a similar point: Alterity is the difference between God and humankind in Christ. But alterity is also human diversity, the interplay of the Same and the Other, *du même et de l'autre.* As Adoukonou has put it, diversity, alterity, must be perceived as gifts — what he calls cultural difference, *la différence culturelle* — gifts given by the One in whom all find community *(l'Identité).* Alterity means that diversity — genuine diversity — is indispensable for those who would understand the incarnation and the crucifixion:

17

The gift of God's self — inseparable from Jesus' suffering — is for the salvation of all.

To draw the African Adoukonou into my discussion of the German Bonhoeffer is to experience alterity, for they embody cultural difference, the one to the other. Racism is rejected in the very synthesis of their positions. After all, they are both *stayed on Jesus!* One can see this in Adoukonou, whom I translate as follows:

> Being by definition hospitable to alterity, theology will be not at all intimidated by difference; to the contrary, it will welcome difference as grace — a gift in service of *la promotion.* Theology lays the ground for the fundamental conditions whereby the free circulation of these gifts, these differences, are possible, for theology is what it is supposed to be as it transgresses its cultural and anthropological *localité,* and sojourns toward the be-all-and-end-all of the Cross, the only historically *given* [emphasis added] utopia looked for today in the dialogue among cultures and religions. (Adoukonou 1980, ix)

At the cross, the vulgar dualism that places the metaphysical demiurge, Racism, in illusory contention with God-in-Christ is exposed as the antithesis of life and health.

The example of Bonhoeffer's life and the legacy of his writings overcome that — the vulgar Manichaeanism of our time: Racism is born from a refusal to accept one God in a unity of persons. "Come what may," sermonized Bonhoeffer during his first trip to the United States, "let us never more forget that one Christian people is the people of God, that if we are in accord, no nationalism, no hate of races or classes can execute its designs, and then the world will have its peace for ever and ever" (NRS, 80). So much for alterity, for now.

As if sin were less rampant today than yesterday, certain Christians suggest that Bonhoeffer's accent on suffering is oppressive. And Bonhoeffer hit that theme pretty hard: "The earthly body of Jesus underwent crucifixion and death. In that death the new humanity undergoes crucifixion and death. Jesus Christ had taken upon him not a man, but the human 'form,' sinful flesh, human 'nature,' so that all whom he bore suffer and die with him" (COD, 266). But even if one exchanges the cross for a symbol free of the association with death — a fecund tree, for instance — it is likely that those bearing such a symbol in contexts sated with injustice will suffer something not unlike crucifixion. When has the world been free of Golgotha-like situations? That racial injustice abounds today all over the world, and that this injustice is in fact killing people by the tens of thousands, itself occasions pain and suffering. Even if one is a world away from the stink of it, how can one fail to mourn?

The suffering to which the world's people are heir brings to light the reality of Bonhoeffer's suffering God. So much is this the case, that I feel bound to say that Christians who would dispense with the cross are living in a fantasy world (and forfeiting their identity). To simply say, *let us downplay the cross, there has been too much emphasis on it,* exposes how far we are from the real world Bonhoeffer embraced. Too much death and dying abound for persons to act as if redemption were won through some virtue (minus the suffering).

When has unfeigned virtue not brought pain and suffering? As I write this I am in Zimbabwe, in Africa (1994); and though Zimbabwe fares better than many African nations, the suffering of the continent at large is very much a reality here. Indigence is a Pan-African reality. In Rwanda, we are witnessing human carnage — the likes of which surely compare in massive human misery to the Holocaust of Bonhoeffer's day. And this carnage — over 500,000 persons dead this year alone, with thousands of bodies dumped in waters that empty in the Nile River, polluting one of the Continent's essential water supplies — reveals the reality of this horror that tells the truth about human beings. There is too much suffering in the "fallen-falling" world not to consider Bonhoeffer's legacy as a viable one.

Yes, Bonhoeffer has much to offer us in regard to his suffering God. As André Dumas, put it (and I paraphrase): Bonhoeffer's simple faith was that God and reality are, in Christ, united polemically in a struggle for abundant life — a war, in which what is truly and unalterably real does not dissolve. As Bonhoeffer saw it, the reality God embraces is the cross; and what does not dissolve is the present-ness of God in Jesus, an invincibility made clear in the resurrection (Dumas 1968, 41). Bonhoeffer keeps one on track, helps one not to miss what my ancestors called the "Gospel train." I admire his conviction that

It is not Christ who must justify Himself before the world by the acknowledgement of the values of justice, truth and freedom, but it is these values which have come to need justification, and their justification can only be Jesus Christ. It is not that a "Christian culture" must make the name of Jesus Christ acceptable to the world; but the crucified Christ has become the refuge and the justification, the protection and the claim for the higher values and their defenders that have fallen victim to suffering. It is with the Christ who is persecuted and who suffers in His Church that justice, truth, humanity and freedom now seek refuge; it is with the Christ who found no shelter in the world, the Christ who was cast out from the world, the Christ of the crib and of the cross, under whose protection they now seek sanctuary, and who thereby for the first time displays the full extent of His power. The cross of Christ makes both sayings true: "He that is not with me is against me" and "He that is not against us is for us." (E, 59)

In this either-or, one's phenotype and genotype are irrelevant. Now *that* is something to die for.

CHAPTER 1

"Lord Help the Poor and Needy":
Rereading Bethge's Dietrich Bonhoeffer

Lord help the poor and needy,
In this land . . .
In this great getting up morning we shall face another sun,
Lord help the poor and needy,
In this land, In this land . . .

Lord help the widows and the orphans, In this land . . .

Lord help the motherless children, In this land . . .

Lord help the hypocrite members, In this land . . .

Lord help the long-tongue liars, In this land . . .

Bonhoeffer loved the spirituals. He wrote:

The most influential contribution made by the Negro to American Christianity lies in the "Negro spirituals," in which the distress

21

and delivery of the people of Israel ("Go down, Moses . . ."), the misery and consolation of the human heart ("Nobody knows the trouble I've seen"), and the love of the Redeemer and longing for the kingdom of heaven ("Swing low, sweet chariot . . .") find moving expression. Every white American knows, sings and loves these songs. It is barely understandable that great Negro singers can sing these songs before packed concert audiences of whites, to tumultuous applause, while at the same time these same men and women are still denied access to the white community through social discrimination. (NRS, 109)

Bonhoeffer thought that contradiction was a symptom of an American religiousness that the majority deemed as ethical and even as the Christian faith.

But, to borrow a bit from Forrest Wood's *The Arrogance of Faith,* was not Christian faith basically American convictions that reflected "the values of American culture at large . . . conservative, provincial, geographically fragmented, locally controlled, and ideologically wrapped up in the dogma of Manifest Destiny" (Wood 1991, 382)? And, as he points out, "trapped at the bottom of all this [have been] the black Americans, many of whom . . . still remember the years when the law did not recognize them as completely human" (384). Bonhoeffer, however, recognized them as human beings because of what had been given him: a faith in God, a faith poetically expressed in African-American spirituals.

I find that the spiritual "Lord Help the Poor and Needy" captures the spirit of Bonhoeffer's life, which I want to explore by following what I find to be the compelling dimensions of Bethge's biography. I will not do this in terms of a triad, as is the case with Bethge, John Godsey, René Marlé, André Dumas, and Hanfried Müller. While I can certainly see the point in distinguishing *The Communion of Saints*–Bonhoeffer from *The Cost of Discipleship*–Bonhoeffer, and that Bonhoeffer from the one of *The Letters and Papers from Prison,* I seek to dovetail the three into the one theme that is this book's raison d'être.

Four parts bring out the antiracist dimensions of Bonhoeffer's life: (1) his commitment to reality, which entails his distinction between faith and religion; (2) his sojourn in Harlem; (3) his desire to study with Gandhi (a desire wed to his rejection of the German, meaning Nazi, Christians); and (4) his struggle against Hitler (a struggle which entailed the distinction between eschatology and creation).

I
Reality

Bonhoeffer scholars (Eberhard Bethge, Ernst Feil, André Dumas [especially Dumas], John Godsey, Clifford Green, Thomas Day) argue that Bonhoeffer favored reality over the metaphysical. The metaphysical is chimera, the mind's fantasy. Reality is God's presence in the world: Bonhoeffer's God is not way up there, somewhere, clicking away unfeelingly like Plotinus's One, but incarnate — worldly. That is — to quote from Bonhoeffer's posthumously published *Ethics* — "It was not metaphysical speculation, it was not a theologumenon of the *logos spermatikos,* but it was the concrete suffering of injustice, of the organized lie, of hostility to mankind and of violence, it was the persecution of lawfulness, truth, humanity and freedom" that drove him to God here and now (E, 58-59). For he found God there, in the midst of such horror.

According to Dumas, Bonhoeffer's embrace of his God and this world was owed to his understanding of the Bible, in which God is found in history. God is the partner in an alliance, which is not simply with the elements, as was the case with Noah — this alliance is historical, as seen in the covenant relationship with Abraham *(avec l'histoire comme en Abraham)* (Dumas 1968, 4). With Noah emphasis is on the deluge — on the hostility of the world to humankind, one might say. But with Abraham one sees that the image of humankind is not the world — at one time effaced underwater — but God. The world is nonetheless part of what is real.

The world, in becoming historical, insofar as the world is the milieu in which Abraham had his being, is humanized *(humanisé)*. The world is, therefore, a theater, in which God *speaks* to humankind. And if God, embracing the world's reality in all of its anthropological and natural dimensions, speaks to Abraham, God *is* this reality in Christ, who is not only word, but *flesh* as well. That, according to Dumas, was Bonhoeffer's faith.

"Faith," Bonhoeffer said, "is a God-given *reality:* one may question its manner of being or becoming, its How, but not the actual fact of its being" (AB, 138). Religion — even if it is "faith-wishfulness" — must, like all penultimate things, dissolve. One should expose its manner of nonbeing, its how, assume that it is false. For religion, Godless to the extent that it is fabricated to promote a selfish happiness, and little else, promotes unhappiness because it is really illusory. One such illusion is racism, whereby happiness is enjoyed at the expense of others.

These others — the African-Americans, and the Holocaust Jews particularly — call to mind God's own unhappiness, for they bring to mind the cross. "With that," wrote Bonhoeffer, in one of his Barcelona sermons that foreshadowed his own martyrdom, "the difference between Christianity and religions is clear; here is grace, there is happiness, here is the cross, there the crown, here God, there man" (Bethge 1985, 80). The point being: God, grace, and cross are nonreligious by virtue of the divine suffering they entail. It is not that suffering is good. To the extent that sin is involved, suffering occurs because people seek a truncated happiness, a crown, at the expense of others. God's own suffering reveals that such happiness is a very one-sided, unrealistic, and self-indulgent view of the world. That is, such illusion is challenged and overcome by "the gift of Christ" — the "grace and the love of God, which reaches its consummation in the cross" (84).

The cross also calls ethics into question. According to Dumas, ethics had two implications for Bonhoeffer — either the dilemmas of the conscience having to do with good and evil, or the recognition of reality reunified *(réunifiée)* by the commandment of God (Dumas 1968, 168). In regard to the former, Bonhoeffer thought human beings were too sinful to know what is good and what bad. In regard to the latter — the reunification of reality that entails the good and the bad — he thought the following. The either-or dichotomy integral to vulgar ethics — one is either good or bad, white or black, in or out — has been overcome in Christ. For nothing summarizes the good and the bad like the antithesis of God and sinful humanity.

Yet Christ, who for Bonhoeffer was both God and man, is so good, and has so reordered the meaning of the bad — having taken sin into God's very own life — that every ethical Thou-shall and Thou-shall-not comes up short. Christ alone was the measure of ethical propriety for Bonhoeffer. Where Christ is not real, ethics are prey to religious manipulation. So faith (reality) and ethics (meaning whether one is in touch with reality) are not identical.

II
Harlem

The distinction is critical if one is to appreciate Bonhoeffer's view of American racism. While Bonhoeffer admired "the capacity of American society for integration and change," the abuse of African-Americans called the United States into question. The abuse itself might be called an ethic: White supremacy has been so much a part of what America is, that all too few Americans are outraged by the fact that a nation founded on the enslavement and continuing mistreatment of blacks is fundamentally unjust. Still, one talks about the American way as a virtuous way, an ethical way, as is attested by the last line of the "Pledge of Allegiance" most American schoolchildren know by heart — "with liberty and justice for all." The Harlem Renaissance poet Langston Hughes has, in his "Children's Rhymes," captured a certain bitterness in that regard:

> By what sends
> the white kids
> I ain't sent:
> I know I can't be President

25

What don't bug
them white kids
sure bugs me:
We knows everybody
ain't free!

What's written down
for white folks
ain't for us a-tall:
"Liberty And Justice —
Huh — For All."

Bonhoeffer conveyed his sense of this American dilemma to his brother Karl-Friedrich, an award-winning physicist, who wrote to Bonhoeffer:

I am delighted you have the opportunity of studying the Negro question so thoroughly. I had the impression when I was over there that it really is *the* problem, at any rate for people with a conscience and, when I was offered an appointment at Harvard, it was a quite basic reason for my disinclination to go to America for good, because I did not want either to enter upon that heritage myself or to hand it on to my hypothetical children. It seems impossible to see the right way to tackle the problem. (Bethge 1985, 110)

Dietrich Bonhoeffer studied *the problem* "through books and count-less visits to Harlem, through participation in Negro youth work, but even more through a remarkable kind of identity with the Negro community, so that he was received there as though he had never been an outsider at all" (114).

In identifying with blacks, Bonhoeffer wrote, "The race question is arriving at a turning-point. The attempt to overcome the conflict religiously or ethically will turn in a violent political objection" (Bethge 1985, 109). It had already begun in 1930 and in 1931 in

Harlem. Adam Clayton Powell, Jr., the son of the senior Powell —
who was pastor of the Abyssinian Baptist Church that Bonhoeffer
attended regularly — mobilized many Harlemites, in order to express their objection. The young Powell "had been involved in a
small way with one group, the Harlem Citizen's Committee for
More and Better Jobs, formed by his father . . . in 1930" (Hamilton
1992, 86).

The struggle has been difficult; for the more that dominant America has rejected, in practice, the proposition that all people are equal
before God, the more blacks have plunged into second-class living
— of one kind or another — with all its inertia and violence. And
the more that blacks have challenged such rejection, struggling all
the while for a fair shake in the land of their birth, the more first-class
citizenship has dodged them. Now that the civil rights and the black
power movements have come and gone, some fifty years after Bonhoeffer immersed himself in Afro-America, the violent objections he
foresaw have resulted in much civil unrest — a tragic black under-
class and a bitterly disappointed black middle class.

In identifying with blacks, in bypassing the ethics and the religion
of a civilization that has rendered them *the problem,* Bonhoeffer —
I say this through hindsight — sought God "in the centre and not
at the borders of reality" (Bethge 1985, 164). The center is where
suffering is, where injustice is. Where suffering and injustice are,
there, also, is God-in-Christ. Failure to see Christ standing in the
middle was, for Bonhoeffer, to follow a fantasy god, a *deus otiose.*
And, asked Bonhoeffer (shortly after he returned to Germany in
1931), "How is one to preach such things to . . . people? Who still
believes them? The invisibility of God breaks us to pieces. . . . This
absurd, perpetual being thrown back on the invisible God — no one
can stand it any longer" (Bethge 1985, 130). No one with faith
believes in a God who is irrelevant to this land. One must be able
to understand, to see, God's reality in the here and now. This seeing
involves the recognition, for Christ's sake, of those who are
oppressed.

27

III
Gandhi

"Every now and then," writes Bethge, "the thought crossed [Bonhoeffer's] mind that India had something to offer that he must investigate" (Bethge 1985, 174). Apparently, he first got the idea of going to Asia in 1928, while he was in Spain. It was an idea planted in him by his paternal grandmother, Julie Bonhoeffer, *née* Tafel. "In your place," she wrote him in a letter, "I should try some time or other to get to know the contrasting world of the East, I am thinking of India, Buddha and his world."

Bethge writes: "It was still a very vague and general thirst for new experience which impelled him to seek contact with a different spiritual world, though he may perhaps already have felt the attraction of the figure of Gandhi. A fellow student at Tübingen recalls a night-time conversation in the winter of 1924-5 in which Gandhi's personality and work already played a part" (1985, 74).

The thought of going to India was likely at the back of Bonhoeffer's mind as he left the United States in 1931. For he had planned "to return home round the other side of the world, by way of India" (Bethge 1985, 107). On the ship that took him to America, in fact, Bonhoeffer talked at length about India with an American, a Dr. Lucas, president of a college in Lahore, India. Lucas invited Bonhoeffer to come to India, where Lucas promised to show him around. Later, though, Bonhoeffer discovered that the trip back to Germany by way of the Pacific would be too expensive. "His mother consoled him. 'I think you will always be able to take leave and visit India from here . . . and be able to go there better prepared and at a more suitable opportunity.'"

In 1932, Bonhoeffer wrote to his friend Erwin Sutz:

I can hardly think of it [his stay in America] without feeling violently attracted by the idea of going abroad again, this time to the East. I don't yet know when. But it cannot be much longer delayed. There must be other people in the world who know more

28

than we do. And in that case it is simply philistine not to go and learn from them. At all events, those people are not the Nazis, and nor are they our communists as I got to know them during the past winter. The Germans are hopelessly set in a fixed direction, in which one can see and know more than the Americans do, but that is not much yet. (Bethge 1985, 174)

And so it was that the ugly rise of nazism gave urgency to Bonhoeffer's desire to study with Gandhi. Let me give a broad view of this development in his life.

As the Nazis gathered steam, around the time Bonhoeffer returned home from the United States, he discovered he had no qualms with the Christians among them on the basis of christology or the Trinity per se. Conceivably, an erudite Nazi could have split hairs as well as any other well-trained theologian regarding anhypostasis and/or enhypostasis, or regarding what is essential and what is economic about a "perichoretic" God. The theological issue for Bonhoeffer was the Nazi Aryan clause.

Adopted in 1933, during the course of the Brown Synod, the Aryan clause rescinded, within the state church (the Evangelical Church in Germany), the orders of pastors of Jewish descent. Most of Germany's Protestants were in that church, a church comprising Lutheran and Reformed traditions. A segment of that church became Nazis and were dubbed the *German* Christians — the champions of the Aryan clause. "That this legislation could have been supported by the German Christians . . . seemed to Bonhoeffer evidence enough that the national church had substituted racial purity for baptism and the call of Christ and had, thereby, fallen into heresy" (Kelly and Nelson 1990, 133). Bonhoeffer refused this drive for racial purity — this *rassenhygiene,* meaning racial hygiene.

In *rassenhygiene,* "weak elements must not be allowed to prosper and, above all, must not be allowed to reproduce" (Shipman 1994, 132). After the Third Reich culled from the master race those whom they considered idiots and cripples, they went after the Jews. The

Aryan clause foreshadowed that, and Bonhoeffer knew it, some six years before the killing started. He saw clearly that any state enshrining racial hygiene as a national law was a sham of a state no God-fearing person was bound to respect. As he argued in his 1933 essay, "The Church and the Jewish Question" — which took the German Christians to task — none wanted lawlessness. But too much law (nazified) encroached upon the church's mandate to uphold God's impartiality to persons.

"Neither Jew nor gentile, neither slave nor free" was the essential thing, as Bonhoeffer saw it, for that was at the heart of "Christian preaching and Christian faith." And it was that to which the Nazis put the screws — a "grotesque situation, as the state only receives its peculiar rights from this proclamation and from this faith, and enthrones itself by means of them." According to Bonhoeffer, "There would be too little law if any group of subjects were deprived of their rights, too much where the state intervened in the character of the church and its proclamation, e.g., in the forced exclusion of baptized Jews from [Protestant] congregations or in the prohibition of . . . mission [sic] to the Jews" (Kelly and Nelson 1990, 139).

Bonhoeffer, then, was in advance of those who saw the Jewish question in terms of *adiaphora*. Meaning "things indifferent," *adiaphora* are inessential to Christian faith; but they might be allowed for the sake of the "weaker brethren." The Reverend Martin Niemöller — a former submarine commander during World War I, whose autobiography, *From U-Boat to Pulpit,* was a hit among the Nazis, and who, according to William Shirer, was initially a Nazi sympathizer — saw the Jewish question as an adiaphoron. Bethge thinks a

comparison of Bonhoeffer's and Niemöller's propositions reveals [Bonhoeffer's view] in spite of the similarity of their actions at [that] time. Niemöller admitted the possibility of reconciling the exclusion of the Jewish Christians from church office with 1 Cor. 8 and the concept of the "weaker brethren." Bonhoeffer, on the other hand, asked "whether, precisely in the cause of the Church the acceptance of such a scandal must not be demanded of the congregation. . . . Those who remain unaffected by that, and hence privileged, will wish to align themselves with their under-privileged brethren rather than make use of privileges within the church." (Bethge 1985, 236)

Taking his cue from Romans 14, Bonhoeffer argued that those who would expel Jews from the church were weak but should not be accommodated, or judged, even though they "had introduced a racial law." He unmasked their view "as a trick of the 'weak' who would like to see their wish become the heretical law of the 'strong'" (Bethge 1985, 219-20).

> Lord help the hypocrite members, In this land . . .
> Lord help the long-tongue liars, In this land . . .

With Hitler's *Reich President's Edict for the Protection of People and State,* a document that marked the Nazi rise to power, Bon-hoeffer became all the more uncooperative with Nazi religion and ethics. "By August 1933, Bonhoeffer was to conclude beyond all doubt that there could be no question of remaining with a church which excluded Jews." He wrote:

> We are in no way concerned with the question whether our members of German stock can continue to share responsibility with Jews for the communion of the Church. Rather, it is the task of the Christian proclamation to say: here, where Jew and German stand together under God's word, is the Church, here it is proven whether or not the Church is still the Church. (Bethge 1985, 207)

Bonhoeffer thought the church had "an unconditional obligation toward the victims of any social order, even where those victims [did] not belong to the Christian community" (208).

Yet, Bonhoeffer, upon the advice of his General Superintendent, backed away from officiating at the funeral of his sister's Jewish father-in-law in 1933, and that haunted him. "I am tormented by the thought," he wrote to his brother-in-law Gerhard Leibholz,

> that I didn't do as you asked me as a matter of course. To be frank, I can't think what made me behave as I did. How could I have been so much afraid at the time? It must have seemed equally incomprehensible to all of you, and yet you said nothing. But it preys on my mind . . . because it's the kind of thing one can never make up for. So all I can do is to ask you to forgive my weakness then. I know now for certain that I ought to have behaved differently. (209)

Bonhoeffer went on to take the church to task for its apathy toward the Aryan clause.

His passion in that made him, along with his partly Jewish friend, Franz Hilderbrandt, odd man out in Germany's Evangelical Church, as both joined the Confessing Church and held to its Barmen Declaration. (The Confessing Church was founded in 1934 and was composed of a small number who had little use for Nazi clergy. They expressed their theology in the Barmen Declaration, which made the difference between the state and the cross clear.)

It bothered Bonhoeffer that many within the Confessing Church were ready to take this oath to Hitler, sworn by many not long after Barmen: "I . . . swear before God . . . that I . . . will be true to the Führer of the German people and State, Adolf Hitler, and I pledge myself to every sacrifice and every service on behalf of the German people such as befit an Evangelical German" (Bethge 1985, 299). *How,* he wondered, *could any one of them think he would show the world the merits of National Socialism?* "Ingenuous visionaries like Niemöller," wrote a pensive Bonhoeffer, "still go on thinking they're the true National Socialists — it may indeed be Providence that has fostered their illusion, and this might even be in the interest of the church" (300).

Bonhoeffer was disillusioned: "He could not and would not remain in relation with men holding ecclesiastical office who had compounded — even unwillingly — with the Nazi Aryan clause. So he wrote farewell letters to them and would not listen to plausible excuses or professions of good intentions" (Bethge 1985, 192). He left Germany in 1933 to pastor a German congregation in England. "He now returned to his former idea of a visit to India, for he wished to become better acquainted with the ethics and practice of passive resistance" (192-93).

From England Bonhoeffer wrote to his brother Karl-Friedrich: "Since I am become daily more convinced that in the West Christianity is approaching its end — at least in its present form, and its present interpretation — I should like to go to the Far East before coming back to Germany" (Bethge 1985, 330). To his very perceptive friend Erwin Sutz, Bonhoeffer wrote: "How long I shall remain a pastor, and how long in this church, I don't know. Possibly not very long. This winter I'd like to go to India" (329-30).

If the Evangelical Church in Germany, Bonhoeffer's church, had become an association of "long-tongue liars" — to make an allusion to the spiritual again — then perhaps that was because it had become "so Westernized and so permeated by civilized thought" as to lose its salt. Surely the Confessing Church, dragging its feet in regards to the Jewish question — and, of course, the strong arm of the Nazis forced many to compromise — had become flat for Bonhoeffer. He was critical of any church, Reich or otherwise, that was unaware of what to do in the height of crisis.

He wrote to his paternal grandmother:

Before I tie myself down anywhere for good, I'm thinking again of going to India. I've given a good deal of thought lately to Indian questions and believe that there's quite a lot to be learnt there. Sometimes it even seems to me that there's more Christianity in their "paganism" than in the whole of our Reich Church. Of course, Christianity did come from the East originally, but it has been so Westernized and so permeated by civilized thought that, as we can now see, it is almost lost to us. Unfortunately I have

33

little confidence left in the church opposition. I don't at all like the way they're going about things, and really dread the time when they assume responsibility and we may be compelled yet again to witness the discrediting of Christianity. I'm not yet absolutely sure how the Indian plan is going to work out. There's a possibility — but please don't mention this to students and so on — that I might go to Rabindranath Tagore's university. But I'd rather go to Gandhi and already have some good introductions from close friends of his. I might be able to stay there for six months or more as a guest. If this is ever arranged and I can manage it financially, I shall go in the winter. (Bethge 1985, 330)

Insightful theologian that he was, Bonhoeffer wished to learn more about the scope of being by studying with the Great Soul, Gandhi. Studying with Gandhi, he would have also deepened his waxing interest in the pacifism to which he was exposed by Jean Lasserre (a Frenchman who was another of Bonhoeffer's best friends during the time he studied at Union).

Gandhi wrote Bonhoeffer a letter of invitation:

With reference to your desire to share my daily life, I may say that you will be staying with me if I am out of prison and settled in one place when you come. But otherwise, if I am traveling or if I am in prison, you will have to be satisfied with remaining in or near one of the institutions that are being conducted under my supervision. If you can live on the simple vegetarian food that these institutions can supply you, you will have nothing to pay for boarding and lodging. (Carter et al. 1991, 209)

Jurjen Wiersma argues that Bonhoeffer was so captive to Western chauvinism as to call Gandhi a "heathen Christian" (Carter et al. 1991, 208). But Wiersma gives no reference for this claim.

That Bonhoeffer, during the course of his sermon on peace — for he realized early on that Hitler meant war — asked his colleagues at the 1934 ecumenical conference at Fäno, Denmark, "Are we to be put to shame by heathens [sic] in the East?" is bothersome indeed (Bethge 1985, 331). I do not think, though, that Bonhoeffer meant to convey the very racist connotation that goes along with dubbing non-Western realities as *heathen*. Certainly, a better translation of this sermon, "The Church and the People of the World," is provided in *A Testament of Hope: The Essential Writings of Dietrich Bonhoeffer,* an excerpt of which reads:

> Why do we fear the fury of the world powers? Why don't we take the power from them and give it back to Christ? We can still do it today. The Ecumenical Council is in session; it can send out to all believers this radical call to peace. The nations are waiting for it in the East and in the West. Must we be put to shame by *non-Christian people in the East* [added]? Shall we desert the individuals who are risking their lives for this message? The hour is late. The world is choked with weapons, and dreadful is the distrust which looks out of every human being's eyes. (Kelly and Nelson 1990, 241)

Non-Christian people is a far better translation than "heathens in the East," for it is in keeping with Bonhoeffer's witness against racism.

That is not to say that Bonhoeffer was free from what Wiersma calls "Western and Euro-centered biases." As I have noted in my Preface, I do not think Bonhoeffer was, entirely. (Who, having been Westernized, is?) But the essential thing is that he clearly struggled against such biases in his willingness to take the realities of the Other seriously: India would have afforded him new vistas similar to those he enjoyed during his Harlem year. It stands to reason, moreover, that Gandhi would have deepened Bonhoeffer's conviction that racism was — and is — a spiritual deformity. For Gandhi's nonviolent way cannot be appreciated in a vacuum: It first took shape during the time Gandhi was a barrister in apartheid South Africa; and this way — this *Satyagraha* — matured in the struggle against British rule in India. How — given Bonhoeffer's character — could he have studied with Gandhi and not have come away from the experience more free from "Euro-centered biases" than before? In sum, the integrity of his intention to edify himself further through more contact with people of color provides direction for racist-free living.

But, as a vociferous, vanguard member of the Confessing Church, Bonhoeffer had to forgo his trip to India. The Nazis had decreed that "theological students were no longer able to take examinations unless they could give proof of their 'Aryan' descent" (Bethge 1985, 333). He could not just abandon the decadent Western church if the Confessing Church might reform it. Could it be that the Confessing Church was en route to realizing that the saints were obligated "not just to bandage the victims [the Jews] under the wheel, but to jam a spoke in the wheel itself"?

At any rate, the wing of the Confessing Church composed of the Old Prussian Council of Brethren felt compelled to train seminarians without regard to their so-called race. Bonhoeffer felt compelled to direct one of these seminaries — Finkenwalde. He believed that when God calls a person, he knows "God alone is concrete . . . [that] the concrete situation is the substance within which the Word of God speaks; it is the object, not the subject, of concretion" (Bethge 1985, 362). Far more important than even the Nazi crisis, for Bonhoeffer, was the Word made flesh in Jesus Christ — "a compelling, dominating Word" (369).

Germany — *the concrete situation* — was the context in which his discipleship had to take form. Bonhoeffer had so wrestled with the implications of his election, that he felt he had *no choice* but to stay in the West; a West hobbled by the illusion of *Rassenhygiene.*

IV
Fighting Hitler

An eschatological theology, a "theology of break-through," which gave substance to his growing opposition to Hitler, was Bonhoeffer's passion now (Bethge 1985, 378). For he found nothing more illusory than creation theologies that legitimized the Nazi's view that "creation" — as interpreted by Ernst Haeckel — meant survival of the fittest. Haeckel, a nineteenth-century biologist, argued that "Jews not only avoided assimilation into German society but were actually biologically incapable of partaking fully of German culture." He was so racist as to have said, "Jesus Christ's father was actually a Roman Officer who had seduced Mary, making Christ only half-Jewish." It was but a small jump to the conclusion that creation itself had no use for the Jews. Hitler himself was taken by Haeckel; very possibly, "the substance and wording of some of Hitler's writing '[emerged] as an extended paraphrase and even at times plagiarism of Haeckel's'" work (Shipman 1994, 134-35).

Bonhoeffer thought the time was ripe for a focus on the fall and the cross, sin and salvation — and in relation to those fast becoming an oxymoron, the German Jews. "To show an interest, however genuine and earnest, in [creation] . . . was to be dangerously near sacrificing at the altar of Hitler" (Bethge 1985, 377). No, Bonhoeffer had to concentrate on an eschatology that made clear just how fallen it was to order, as in rank, the world under the scepter of the swastika. This had to be done "so that the whole of this earth may be reconquered by the illimitable message" — what has been given us (378). Illimitable, because nonreligious, this break-through message — that God is no respecter of persons — was borne by a minority. Only true believers realized the time had come to assert Christ over the abusive power of a very racist state, which entailed an appreciation of the distinction between creation and preservation.

According to Bonhoeffer: "*Creation* means wresting out of non-being; *preservation* means confirmation of being. *Creation* is real *beginning*, always 'before' my knowledge and before *preservation*" (CF, 26). Before humankind had been saddled with its sin — long before the ugliness of the Holocaust — it would have been okay to say in one breath, "creation *and* preservation." Both would have been owed to God's good graces, for both would have been "related to the same object, the original good work of God." But with Nazis goose-stepping all over the place, one had to see "the preservation of the original creation and the preservation of the fallen creation are two entirely different things" (CF, 26). One had to understand what death meant (and means) — not our biological end as much as a consequence of sin, which entails the wanton killing of unwanted human beings. It

> began in 1939 with retarded or handicapped children under the age of three who were confined to institutions. They died by injections, poisoning, gassing, slow starvation, or even exposure when institutions were not heated, but they died mostly at the hands of medical professionals. Most sinister of all is the fact that these physicians and nurses were not *ordered* to kill patients; they were simply *empowered* to do so. The killing soon spread to adult psychiatric patients; some 70,273 were killed by 1941. Rumors of the killings grew to the point that some elderly refused to enter retirement homes, fearing those would be the next target. (Shipman 1994, 138)

Rassenhygiene grew out of a people who thought themselves a *peuple démiurge* (a demiurge people) indeed. As I have noted, the cleansing began with their own throw-away folk; and this too bears reiteration: "Once the link was made between those who were genetically defective (in the sense of bearing physical or mental handicaps) and euthanasia, it was a simple matter to extend the principle to justify elimination of the Jews" (138). Bonhoeffer's quest for a breakthrough theology sought to fight that sinful reality.

His resolve was so strong that he rejected outright the 1938 oath to Hitler. ("I swear that I will be faithful and obedient to Adolf Hitler, the Führer of the German Reich and people, that I will conscientiously observe the laws and carry out the duties of my office so help me God.") That the Confessing Church, especially his wing of it, the Old Prussian Confessional Synod, "decided in favor of the oath ... when it already knew that a regulation was coming by which non-Aryans were compelled to have a large 'J' stamped on their identity cards" shamed Bonhoeffer (Bethge 1985, 507). He wondered:

What is to be done? Swearing the oath will irrevocably take place in the next couple of days and the synod will be responsible for it. Many consciences will have been burdened by this. Humanly speaking, one can never make amends for the disruption that has been caused in the Confessing Church. That is the special seriousness of this matter of the oath. I can view the guilt that the Confessing Church has burdened itself with through the directive on taking the oath only as the consequence of a way of life in which the lack of full power, of joy in confessing, of courage in faith, and of readiness for suffering has already become noticeable among us for quite a long time. The fact cannot be hidden that this means a difficult temptation for many parishioners and pastors. What will we learn from this? (Kelly and Nelson 1990, 489)

Together with the fact that he might be drafted into the Nazi army, the question was a contributing factor leading Bonhoeffer back to New York City.

He arrived in 1939. While he was more appreciative of the Americans in 1939 than he had been in 1930, he found, overall, that American Christians were too content with "a relativizing of the question of truth." *He* had to decide, in a given time and a specific context, what the truth was. The Americans — with no christology to speak of — could not help him. He *had* to go home. As he put it in a letter to Reinhold Niebuhr:

I have made a mistake in coming to America. I must live through this difficult period of our national history with the Christian people of Germany. I will have no right to participate in the reconstruction of Christian life in Germany after the war if I do not share the trials of this time with my people. . . . Christians in Germany will face the terrible alternative of either willing the defeat of their nation in order that Christian civilization may survive, or willing the victory of their nation and thereby destroying our civilization. I know which of these alternatives I must

39

choose; but I cannot make that choice in security. (Bethge 1985, 559)

Several factors influenced Bonhoeffer in his decision and bear on America's racial dilemma.

These factors are recorded in an essay Bonhoeffer wrote in 1939 entitled "Protestantism without Reformation," which sheds additional light on his earlier view that America's race problem cannot be solved religiously or ethically. Again, religion and ethics in America only fortify racism; and Bonhoeffer suggests this is because church and society — the stated separation between them notwithstanding — are confused in the United States. The confusion takes one to the very founding of the nation:

> Here lies the key to the understanding of the original significance of the American separation of church and state, and of the American Constitution. . . . *American democracy is founded not on humanity or on the dignity of man, but on the kingdom of God and the limitation of all earthly power.* (NRS, 102)

The fact that such democracy functioned at the expense of African and Native American peoples meant that this American view of the kingdom had all too little to do with faith. And that is why, to quote Bonhoeffer, *"The race question* has been a real problem for American Christianity from the beginning." For any nation that thinks itself the kingdom of God, and is dependent on the enslavement of an entire people, has confused faith with a form of New World religion:

> *The American separation of church and state does not rest on the doctrine of the two offices or of the two realms,* which will remain ordained by God until the end of the world, each with its own duty fundamentally different from the other. . . . The interplay of state and church becomes a relationship of subordination in which the state is merely the executive of the church. (NRS, 103)

How easy it was, then, to sanction slavery as the will of God and as the foundation of democracy.

A slave-holding nation, however, misunderstands the very character of freedom. For:

> *The freedom of the church is not where* it *has possibilities, but only where the Gospel really and in its own power makes room for itself on earth, even and precisely when no such possibilities are offered it.* (NRS, 100, emphasis added)

That is, the church's freedom is not the assumption that an American view of the world is in fact God's illimitable grace: "The essential freedom of the church is not a gift of the world to the church, but the freedom of the Word of God itself to gain a hearing." And I venture to say that this word of God — that Bonhoeffer called "a must," "a necessity," an irresistible imperative against all one-sided possibility — condemns racism. For racism cannot help but to misconstrue the world in trying to abort the God-given possibilities for freedom for *all* people.

Because Americans have confused the state, and the church, with God's kingdom, and thought that freedom pertained to whites alone, Bonhoeffer, despite his abiding appreciation for the social gospel movement, concluded his "Protestantism without Reformation" as follows:

> American theology and the American church as a whole have never been able to understand the meaning of "criticism" by the Word of God and all that signifies. Right to the last they do not understand that God's "criticism" touches even religion, the Christianity of the churches and the sanctification of Christians, and that God has founded his church beyond religion and beyond ethics. . . . In American theology, Christianity is still religion and ethics. But because of this, the person and work of Jesus Christ must, for theology, sink into the background and in the long run remain misunderstood, because it is not recognized as the sole

41

ground of radical judgement and radical forgiveness. The decisive task for today is the dialogue between Protestantism without Reformation and the churches of the Reformation. (NRS, 113)

This dialogue must also include a conversation with the black church.

According to Dumas, the one place Bonhoeffer found Protestantism *with* Reformation was at the Abyssinian Baptist Church in Harlem. For, as Dumas points out, it was in Harlem alone, among the piety, and the charisma, and the theology of the shouting blacks *(dans la piété des Noirs, dans leur cultes et leur théologie)* that Bonhoeffer discovered the very *christianisme de la Réformation,* in fact. The white church, however *(la religion officielle en Amérique),* seemed to Bonhoeffer but a social event *(lui paraissait plutôt un événement social)* (Dumas 1968, 53).

In sum, America's widespread theological immaturity was a decisive factor in pushing Bonhoeffer back home to his fate. *Steal away, steal away, steal away to Jesus* — goes a spiritual Bonhoeffer might have hummed — *I ain't got long to stay here.*

Back in Germany, Bonhoeffer, with Martin Niemöller, Hans von Dohnanyi, General Hans Oster, and others, joined the conspiracy to assassinate Hitler. Toward that end, he worked within the Department of Military Intelligence, the *Abwehr.* Using this official connection, as if he were a clergyperson in service to Hitler, he made good on his ecumenical contacts in order to drum up Allied support for the projected coup. His cover was so convincing — who would have thought *Bonhoeffer* worked for the *Abwehr?* — that Karl Barth himself wondered about Bonhoeffer: "Could it be right and proper for anyone like Bonhoeffer, a Confessing pastor who was banned by the Gestapo, to cross the Swiss frontier, with valid papers in the middle of the war? How did he come to do that? Could it be that, after all the German victories, even Bonhoeffer had changed his mind?" (Bethge 1985, 631-32).

In his "official visits" to places such as Switzerland, Bonhoeffer apprised influential clergy such as Barth, Visser 't Hooft, and Bishop Bell of the planned coup d'état, with the hope that the Allies would cease fire in its wake, and support the emergency, monarchist government that would follow. Having left the "relativizing" world of North America, he took his own relativizing world to task, sure that it brought about the Nazi *débâcle*. "He accepted," writes Bethge, "the weight of that collective responsibility, and began to identify himself with those . . . prepared to answer for guilt and tentatively to shape something new for the future, instead of merely protesting on ideological grounds, as had hitherto been usual on the ecclesiastical plane" (Bethge 1985, 581). While involved in espionage, Bonhoeffer continued right on with his official ties to the Confessing Church — counseling the Finkenwalde brothers, most of whom were killed in battle; upholding the principles of the Barmen and Dahlem synods; making theological sense of a communion of saints that increasingly functioned as a rag-tag army.

> I ain't got time for to stop and talk,
> The road is rough and it's hard to walk.
> And I will die in the field . . .
> I'm on my journey home.

So goes another spiritual that calls to mind Bonhoeffer's spirit. The Nazis' war against the world called for a certain martial approach to action. For the sake of the poor and needy, the widows and the orphans, in his land, the realistic Christian, as opposed to the religious Christian, had no choice but to confront Hitler head-on. Religious platitudes, though they be erudite, were to be cast aside by those who knew what to *do*.

As Bonhoeffer saw it, "Christ neither removes reality nor makes it 'Christian'" (Bethge 1985, 624). Reality involves the realization of a yes-and-no, a what-is-right and what-is-wrong — in this land. Neither the Jews nor the death camps were Christian; but neither were those who went to church and turned a deaf ear to the Jews' lamentations. It was important to see that reality and to see that the call to the Christian life meant the unqualified rejection of a nazified nation.

"If we claim to be Christian," said Bonhoeffer, allegedly to his friend, mentor, and *bon confident* Bishop Bell, "there is no room for expediency. Hitler is the Antichrist. Therefore we must go on with our work and eliminate him whether he be successful or not" (Bethge, 626-27). Although Bonhoeffer thought that Hitler was too asinine to be the Devil — so it is unlikely that he referred to Hitler as the Antichrist — he surely thought Hitler was the antithesis of Christ, refused to see Hitler in Christian terms, and recognized Christ did not displace, or sanctify, the Axis reality.

"I pray," he wrote, "for the defeat of my country, for I think that it is the only possibility of paying for all the suffering my country has caused in the world" (Bethge 1985, 648). So resolute was Bonhoeffer in this that he was willing to kill Hitler himself, even if he had to resign from the ministry and from his church altogether. But Bonhoeffer neither planted nor transported the bombs in the failed assassination attempts against the *Führer*. Neither did he put the church so behind him as to be visionless as to its reorganization. "On the contrary, the break for worldly business . . . freed him for what needed to be done in the church's spiritual field" (Bethge 1985, 679). Still, Bonhoeffer fully accepted the possibility that his church would renounce him after his role in the conspiracy came to light.

For that role, he was arrested. Faith (costly grace, reality) brought him to Tegel prison in 1943. The upper-crust, erudite gentleman and accomplished pianist found himself far from middle-class life. As I have noted in my Preface, Bonhoeffer enjoyed a little clout in prison; and several guards thought highly of him, respected his calling, admired his principles, were comforted by the way he acted as a pastor even to them. But he was still beset by the indignities of prison life — "the meager food, the dirt, the ruffians with the keys and the humiliation of the handcuffs" (Bethge 1985, 734).

The dashed expectations of release, a foiled escape, separation from his fiancée, the flu-like sicknesses, the rheumatism, the stomach pains that continued to weaken his body were all elements that tended to dampen his spirit. Materially, psychologically, emotionally, those deprivations made up the reality of one who obeyed a crucified God. Bonhoeffer was not special in this: in today's world the number of justice-loving folk incarcerated for political reasons, and who are suffering because of it, is huge. But Bonhoeffer's misery substantiates his nonreligious interpretation: "Before God and with God," he wrote while in prison, "we live without God." As do many deprived people, for whom daily life is a challenge, Bonhoeffer realized that "keep the faith" is more than a cliché.

Think again about the African-Americans he encountered some thirteen years before in Harlem. Contemplate their spirituals that Bonhoeffer loved, which indicate that faith is, certainly, evidence of things unseen: God does not break into history like High John the Conqueror — a mighty Titan storming over the ocean waters, a man taller than the Atlantic is deep, whom the slaves conjured as a symbol of deliverance. There was no such god for Bonhoeffer or for certain African-Americans, who believed in redemption and the cross in the way that Bonhoeffer did.

The implications of the redeeming cross put one in the mind of a plaintive melody,

> I've been 'buked and I've been scorned . . .
> I've been talked about sure's you born.
>
> There is trouble all over this world,
> There is trouble all over this world . . .
>
> Ain't going to lay my religion down, no!
> Ain't going to lay my religion down . . .

While the word "religion" here appears to contradict the prevailingly negative sense Bonhoeffer gave to it, the spiritual has a lot going for it as far as Bonhoeffer is concerned. Its simplicity, the repetition of simple lines, "I've been 'buked, I've been scorned; there is trouble all over this world," makes the point. No escape from reality — from unmerited suffering, from unwarranted calumny, from an unjust world. *But,* "I ain't going to lay my religion down": no matter what, I will not capitulate to unGodly forces, for my belief is that faith is found in one strong enough to withstand such reproach, such mockery, such affliction. *Ain't going to be no other way.*

"So," wrote Bonhoeffer while in prison,

> our coming of age leads us to a true recognition of our situation before God. God would have us know that we must live as [persons] who manage our lives without him. The God who is with us is the God who forsakes us (Mark 15.34). The God who lets us live in the world without the working hypothesis of God is the God before whom we stand continually. Before God and with God we live without God. God lets himself be pushed out of the world on to the cross. He is weak and powerless in the world, and that is precisely the way, the only way, in which he is with us and helps us. Matt. 8.17 makes it quite clear that Christ helps us, not by virtue of his omnipotence, but by virtue of his weakness and suffering. (LPP, 360-61)

The religionless God, the Other beyond the metaphysical hypothesis, is the one whom Bonhoeffer thought had asked him, "Who do You say that I am?" And Bonhoeffer, having really wanted to know "who Christ really is, for us today," came to see that "only the suffering God can help" (361).

He saw in prison how different faith is from "the shallow and banal this-worldliness of the enlightened, the busy, the comfortable, or the lascivious." Faith gave rise to a "profound this-worldliness, characterized by discipline and the constant knowledge of death and resurrection" (Bethge 1985, 772-73). Faith corrected for Bonhoeffer "the unquenchable urge of [humankind] to glorify, deify or demonize its progress, and, today perhaps even more necessarily in the other direction, protect[ed] the rationalist from [the] unfortunate tendency to the sterile fragmentation of . . . pessimistic resignation and skeptical agnosticism" (773).

To leave things in the shadows of Golgotha, then, would have abbreviated the gospel's message. Resurrection — eschatological — theology also had a place in Bonhoeffer's mind and in his heart. Racism's ugliness hardly consumed him. Joy was a big factor in Bonhoeffer's nonreligious interpretation as well. He refused, for instance, to succumb to the thoughts of suicide that plagued him when he thought he might play the stool pigeon upon being tortured. He fought his *accidie* and his *tristitia,* an overall graveyard feeling that numbs one's resolve to live with vim and vigor. Bonhoeffer had hope; and the good things God created gave him real respite from his troubles: sunshine, fragrant flowers in spring, a loving letter from his wife-to-be, Maria.

Poet at heart, he could write from his cell — "a room seven feet by ten with a plank bed, a bench along the wall, a stool and a bucket, a plank door with an observation hole to look in from the outside and a garret window above his head on the other side" —

> Loyal hearts can change the face of sorrow,
> softly encircle it with love's most gentle
> unearthly radiance.

Well loved by family, friends, inmates, and guards, he kept the faith because he realized "it is only when one loves life and the earth so much that without them everything seems to be over that one may believe in the resurrection and a new world . . ." (LPP, 157). Bonhoeffer's *joie de vivre* was the fruit of his refusal to relegate God to heaven alone, his refusal to push God out of the world through personal, atomistic, legalistic longing for "a long white robe."

There is trouble all over this world: Genuine joy has no stock with an inwardness that flees the world, that truncates redemption in assuming that only people "just like me" go to heaven. Exclusive churches of that mettle shrivel into ecclesial ghettos. And that meant that a racist church was "on the defensive. No taking risks for others"

(Bethge 1985, 779). Especially not the Jews. Where the bluest I reigned — Aryans only. (And in America that meant: all "Negroes" to the back of the bus.) As Bethge put it, Bonhoeffer believed that racist Christianity had become "'law,' . . . the condition of salvation — one must belong to it. Religion has become essentially a way of distinguishing people. A victim of its divisive privileged character, it has presided over a vast number of acts of violence throughout history: Christian against non-Christians, theists against atheist, or whites against coloured people" (780).

Shuffled from prison to prison — en route to Flossenbürg, where he was hanged — Bonhoeffer's situation deteriorated toward the end of the war. Unlike his also-imprisoned brother, Klaus, and brother-in-law, Hans von Dohnanyi, Dietrich was not tortured. But he was subjected to "repulsive" cross-examinations as the Nazis pieced together the details of the conspiracy. He was found out; sentenced to death. On the way to the gallows he said: "This is the end — for me the beginning of life." Before his hanging, he prayed humbly and fervently. His brother and brother-in-law, along with other conspirators, were executed too.

What is more illusory than death for one who has seen, and really seen, Christ? And what more nonreligious than the death of one who dies for Christ's sake? Bonhoeffer thought his death was the way from reality to reality *(from God to God)*. Among his final insights: "Joy is hidden in suffering, and life in death." Death, despite the lacunae it leaves as our inheritance, is a metaphor for God's presence. And this metaphor, if we take reality seriously, points us to life indeed — at least to Bonhoeffer's life before his death. Because of how he lived and why he died, one wants to know more of him: One does not resist racism as Bonhoeffer did because he or she wants a reward in "heaven." To stand up for what is right, concretely in the here and now, is enough.

In the wake of his death, I would like to examine, in the chapters that follow, the depth of his stand-up-for-what-is-right legacy, an antiracist legacy. What better way to appreciate Luther's dictum:

"Living, but no, rather dying and being damned, constitutes the theologian, but not understanding, reading and speculating." For reality has to do with how we should live, and thus how we should think, if we are to know what to do, and — what has been given us . . . in this land.

CHAPTER 2

Old Time Religion:
Rereading The Communion of Saints and
Act and Being — Bonhoeffer's Early Theology

Give me that old time religion,
it's good enough for me . . .

It was good for Paul and Silas . . .

Makes me love everybody . . .

It's good when I'm in trouble . . .

It will do when I am dying . . .

It will take us all to heaven . . .

It should be clear by now that Bonhoeffer thought religion was mostly flight from the living God and from Godless men. Religious Christians, with yellow streaks down their backs, had nothing to offer an aggressive and Godless world, in which Christianity was but hallowed superstition. What mattered to him — it bears frequent reiteration — was faith: a tough, worldly love, and a durable, real-life gracefulness, which opposed racist illusion. The spiritual "Old Time Religion" suggests that, behind its lyrics — its understanding, its *clinging to God's promise* — is a faith similar to Bonhoeffer's: a determination to live in defiance of injustice. *It is good when I'm in trouble. . . . It will do when I am dying. . . . It will take us all to heaven.* (It was surely good enough for Bonhoeffer that fateful day in Flossenbürg.) Although it appears that Bonhoeffer experienced his faith only after his sojourn in Harlem — Bethge says "a change took place in [Bonhoeffer]" after Harlem, as if he were born again — he had before then a cerebral relationship with his faith that he understood in terms of the church, "a community of persons." One sees this clearly in his doctoral dissertations, *The Communion of Saints* and *Act and Being,* which lend substance to the fact that Bonhoeffer did the right thing in Harlem, and in fighting the Nazis.

I
The Communion of Saints

Sociology — which "may . . . be defined as the study of the structures of communities and the acts of will that constitute them" — is a means by which Bonhoeffer stresses the reality, the empirical-ness, of the church in *The Communion of Saints* (SC, 53). For sociology — "the science of the structures of empirical communities" — looks at "the laws" governing those communities as entities in themselves. By virtue of attention to empirical structure alone, sociology "seeks to grasp in empirical acts the essential constitutive acts."

Thus, "Sociology is concerned with tracing the manifold interactions to specific spiritual and intellectual acts of our being which are the peculiar characteristics of the structure." As opposed to social philosophy, sociology — in investigating and recording what sets one group apart from another in space and in time — can be divested of metaphysics and thereby serve the theologian's analysis of the church's concrete structure (1920).

Taking his cue from Ernst Troeltsch's view of modern sociology as "analytic and formal," Bonhoeffer sought to make faith — what has been given us in the church — intelligible in terms of *specific relations* and *social forces*. Social forces entail "love, subordination, mystery, conflict"; specific relations — that is, "kind of relations" — entail the distinction between community and society. The two of them together, specific relations and social forces, influence "the products of society, such as culture, economic life, and 'materializing of the objective spirit'" (SC, 16). For what a community and a society are, as well as how "love, subordination, mystery, conflict" are experienced within them, is related to the structure that gives them a certain identity — an objective spirit — "the . . . spiritual principle springing from socialisation" (SC, 144).

As a thing apart from the willing subjects within it, the objective spirit indicates the way a people love, organize themselves, resolve conflict, express their dilemmas (SC, 65). This can be dangerous: "The objective human spirit is a prey to the historical ambiguity of all profane communities, of all so-called ideal social groups, vain, extravagant, and mendacious" (SC, 149).

All these things, all of these *interactions* — kinds of relations, social forces, products of society, objective spirit — help Bonhoeffer answer the questions, What makes human beings who they are? Are they determined by the play of social forces and specific relations merely? Do such factors determine what a community is? And, What does all this mean for the church? My questions are: If *society's* reigning ethos is a racist one, are *communities* bound to be racist? Are *persons*, therefore, bound to be racists? And how does Bonhoeffer provide a few answers: How did *The Communion of Saints* prepare him to confront racism?

Given the witness of his life in Harlem and rejection of the Aryan clause, Bonhoeffer did not accept that the meaning of human life was so arbitrary as to be bound by bigoted forces unleashed by human society. If that were true, whatever love there is, whatever mystery, whatever conflict too, would be due to impersonal (God-less) forces — so determinative of social existence as to rule out *community,* without which there is no *church*.

The sociological form of the church involves three "elements": God, person, community — which Bonhoeffer calls the "basic ontic relations of social being as a whole." What is more, "It is in relation to persons and personal community that the concept of God is formed": To say "God" is to say community as well as person, as neither community nor persons are really present without God (SC, 22).

Social philosophies — the genealogy of which is fourfold in *The Communion of Saints* — cannot do justice to Bonhoeffer's God-centered sociology. They cannot adequately show us why a person has both an individual and a collective dimension, which interact in making one a social being in tune with the reality of God. Such philosophies — Aristotle's, the Stoics', the Epicureans', and the Enlightenment's, particularly Kant's — do not know what it means to be a person, or to be in relationships with other persons (despite their so-called race). They cannot, therefore, explain what it means to be in relation to God.

The only philosophy that Bonhoeffer thinks serves as a guide to community is "a Christian social philosophy." It begins with the realization that one never attains an appreciation of the Other, i.e., "alien subjects," from "the purely transcendental category of the universal" — from an abstract starting point (SC, 28). If a Christian encounters the Other concretely, he/she acknowledges the impene-trability of the Other — the alien-ness that nurtures community because it is, itself, what is inviolate about sociality: the given, un-impeachable enigma of the Other's subjective self.

"How then do we reach the alien subjects?" asks Bonhoeffer. "By knowledge there is no way at all, just as there is no way by pure knowledge of God" (SC, 28). Persons, alien subjects, cannot be objectified. To objectify them, as racists tend to objectify those they think are beneath them, is to lose touch with reality. Not only is the object an illusion, but the one who refuses, sinfully, to yield to another's subjectivity has forfeited community.

The late Ralph Ellison, a well-respected African-American writer, makes a similar point in his *Shadow and Act.* The white mind in America, he writes, had so objectified the African-American that "he could appear only with his hands gloved in white and his face blackened with burnt cork or greasepaint." The reality of the one so caricatured was "unimportant, the mask was the thing (the 'thing' in more ways than one) and its function was to veil the humanity of Negroes thus reduced to a sign, and to repress the white audience's awareness of its moral identification with its own acts and with the human ambiguities pushed behind the mask" (Ellison 1972, 49). In short, the mask exemplifies Bonhoeffer's view that "so long as [a certain] mind is dominant, and claims universal validity, so long as all *contradictions* [emphasis added] that may arise with the perception of a subject as an object of knowledge are thought of as immanent in my mind, I am not in the social sphere" (SC, 28-29).

As Bonhoeffer knew well, whites and blacks have surely not been in the same social sphere because the dominant society has refused — in repressing "awareness of its moral identification with its own acts and with the human ambiguities pushed behind" the comic Other — to treat blacks as alien subjects worthy of respectful acknowledgment. Society has been in the dark regarding the meaning of Bonhoeffer's "Christian philosophy" — human bonding of the most inspired kind; no distancing racism, which makes of others but a deformed image of the self, is appropriate. Real community does not reduce the alien person's inward self to caricature.

Bonhoeffer's Christian philosophy entails a *barrier* — which is at once the alien subject's incontrovertible uniqueness and the refusal to try to domesticate such uniqueness. Where racism thrives, the barrier is

not acknowledged. This [acknowledgment] is only possible in the ethical sphere; this does not mean, however, that the barrier must have only an ethical content. . . . It can be purely intellectual, that is, it can be experienced, for instance, in the conflict of perceptions. But the experience of the barrier as real is of a specifically ethical character. (SC, 29)

Only in the ethical sphere, then — where one does or does not respect differences — does life with the mysterious Other become reality, or illusion.

Bonhoeffer's barrier brings the dissonance of jazz music to mind. The distinctive voices of the musicians — for each artist plays a different rhythm — are greatly esteemed. Neutralize such distinctions — meaning the dissonance — and destroy the creative impression that is the ensemble itself. That would not be ethical; for dissonance is more than music; it is also a way of life that enjoys diversity and spontaneity — the beauty and rightness of which is the poetry and magic of the music itself.

Within the tight-knit band, failure to assert one's self, to "solo" — or playing in a way that steps on the toes of others — hamstrings this very unique form of "life together." A destructive musician, then — to quote Bonhoeffer heuristically — believes he has "command of his own ethical value, entered by his own strength into the ethical sphere, and [has borne] his ethical motives within himself, as a person equipped with mind" (SC, 29). While Bonhoeffer's remarks are, at first glance, more pertinent to his views on the Categorical Imperative — Kant's "You can, for you ought" — than to jazz, the analogy of the jazz band is nonetheless apt. For, it "is the concept of reality which must be discussed"; and what, after all, is closer to the truth — such an imperative (as theoretical as it is), or this music styled from the real-life suffering of persons? Truly, the person equipped with mind is not on par with the one equipped with what jazz musicians call *feeling*.

James Baldwin captures what I am trying to say in his short story "Sonny's Blues." Toward the end of the story, Baldwin describes a jazz pianist's, Sonny's, performance. Struggling with the terrors of racism, Sonny had not played in a year and so was out of sync with his sibling-musicians: "He and the piano stammered, started one way, got scared, stopped; started another way, panicked, marked time, started again. . . ." How to bring Sonny into the community? Creole, the bassist, "without an instant's warning . . . started into something else, it was almost sardonic, it was *Am I Blue*":

> The dry, low, black man said something awful on the drums, Creole [the bassist] answered, and the drums talked back. Then the horn insisted, sweet and high, slightly detached perhaps, and Creole listened, commenting now and then, dry, and driving, beautiful and calm and old. Then they all came together again, and Sonny was part of the family again. . . . He seemed to have found, right there beneath his fingers, a damn brand new piano. (Baldwin 1995, 138-39)

Feeling-persons experience a spiritual communication with others, listen to others, give them space to be, to be heard — "For, while the tale of how we suffer, and how we are delighted, and how we may triumph is never new, it always must be heard."

Feeling-persons are in touch with others within a dissonant community that nurtures personhood by freeing individuals of the illusion of self-sufficiency. Rather than to "try to figure people out" as objects of knowledge, one fosters social relations, not asocial ones. An asocial jazz musician, in actual performance, is an oxymoron, for, in objectifying his fellow artists all too subjectively, he fails to yield to them — fails to be with them. Should one fail to be with others — forsaking the example of Creole's being with Sonny — he or she truncates the real world; fails to see that the Other — to draw from Bonhoeffer's critique of Kant — "is not the idealist's reasoning person or personified mind, but a particular living person." The time to be with the Other is now — on the beat! — for she or he has "a dynamic and not a static character" (SC, 30). No timeless ethical imperatives are given, only the urgency of the conflict-laden moment. In the exigency of that moment, one, aided by a "Christian philosophy," must know what to do, because of who the Other is.

Consider, for example, Bonhoeffer's friendship with the African-American Frank Fisher. Theirs was no easy friendship; "it continually had to be reconsolidated." The centuries-long enmity between whites and blacks in North America had made "I-Thou" relationships between the two a challenge, to say the least. Genuine fraternity is nonetheless precisely predicated on Bonhoeffer's realization: The "Thou . . . is not an I in the sense of the I-Thou relation." The Thou's I, the alien I, is unknowable — someone apart from the mutual ground that is the I-Thou relation. Bonhoeffer would never know what it meant to be *Frank* Fisher; neither would Fisher know what it meant to be *Dietrich* Bonhoeffer. "But," writes Bethge, "Dietrich Bonhoeffer was an artist in offering unqualified friendship." I believe he was an artist because he had really studied the dissonant art of being-in-community in *The Communion of Saints.* So when, in the racist New World, the time came for him to practice what he preached, he knew what to do.

"In a restaurant on one occasion, for instance, when it was made plain that Fisher was not going to receive the same service as the other customers, [Fisher and Bonhoeffer] ostentatiously walked out" (Bethge 1985, 113-14). His action was no mean feat when you consider what Bonhoeffer would do in regard to the Aryan clause; his disdain for America's double standard foreshadowed what he would do when the chips were down back home. Both in racist America and in racist Germany, Bonhoeffer's actions have shown that he paid more than lip-service to the claim he made in his first doctoral dissertation: "the Thou-form is to be defined as the *other* who places before me a moral decision," his (i.e., Fisher's) enigma notwithstanding (SC, 33-34, emphasis added). The theological implications of this moral decision are exceeding rich.

To assume, tacitly, that God is I and not Thou — which given Bonhoeffer's theo-sociology would mean that the other person would be what *I* need him to be — is to veer from God's path — the only moral path. This is because one, in assuming that he or she knows God's I, confuses God with the self. But God's I is impenetrable, and this opacity is the ground of the neighbor's inviolate, inward self. To transgress the neighbor's inner sanctum, based on your aversion to what is epiphenomenal — in this case the color of his skin — is akin to blasphemy.

It is blasphemy by virtue of the *imago Dei,* for "every human Thou is an image of the divine Thou" (SC, 36). That Bonhoeffer believed this goes to the heart of the issue: God's image is not epidermal. Having nothing to do with lips and hair, totally irrelevant to the bluest eye, God's image pertains to whether a person is good. That goodness alone determines whether individuals realize that God is discovered in the unqualified goodwill each person extends to others: The *imago Dei* is the holiness of a person and the sanctity of the I-Thou community of which he or she is a part. God's image is thus eminently social, discovered more in the collective Thou than the atomistic I — which precludes the bigoted community because "the Thou of God, [is] the absolute will . . . visible in the concrete Thou of social life" (36). That, surely, was the witness of Bonhoeffer's life in Harlem. Bethge writes, "In view of the delicacy of personal relationships between black and white in the United States, Bonhoeffer was surprisingly successful in becoming a welcome guest in the homes of the outcasts of Harlem. He had a gift of restoring the pride and self-confidence of the vulnerable and the sensitive" (1985, 114). It is inconceivable to me, however, that one man, no matter how gifted, could restore something that has never been lost really. African-Americans have never been so oppressed as to have neither pride nor confidence. Sameness only makes it seem so. Nor have they been so broken — terrorized, yes — as to be as vulnerable and as sensitive as abused children. No. I suspect Bonhoeffer was welcomed in Harlem because he carried himself like a pilgrim on the way. Otherwise Harlem would not have been so hospitable. Yes: a pilgrim on the way — a Thou-in-the-image-of-God — a reserved but humble man *leaning on the Lord;* someone who understood the words of a spiritual,

> You got shoes
> I got shoes
> All God's children got shoes

When I get to heaven
going to put on my shoes
And walk all over God's heaven

I got shoes, Thou got shoes: the challenge is to live as though it were so on earth as it is in heaven. The I-Thou community, though now pockmarked with sinfulness, is the foundation of Bonhoeffer's Christian "philosophy" that is reflected in the dogma about humankind's "original spirituality in a state of integrity" (SC, 39).

In the Beginning, before sin, mortals followed God's direction innocently; so "there can be no objection to describing this freely affirmed direction as morality and religion." In the freedom God had originally given, one's sense of God's good graces might also be said to have been metaphysical: God did not — and does not — so totalize human persons that they were forbidden the "unity of self-conscious and spontaneously active spirit" (SC, 39). That is, in the Beginning — when one was free from the enmity toward God that has caused atrocities such as the Middle Passage — the concept of the person was "universal-spiritual-metaphysical" rather than ethical. In that primal state, *the* barrier — the vertical one between Creator and creature — had not been breached nor dissonance leveled. There was "immediate community" between God and humankind. Sociality was "based purely on persons."

But, asserts Bonhoeffer, all that is irrelevant from a Christian perspective. To focus on the primal Beginning is ahistorical. One who takes the world seriously realizes that history is in part a tragic record of sin and death. Similarly, one who takes God seriously realizes that one can overcome this sin because of the Savior. In no sense, however, does this betterment of the human condition reproduce the Beginning — the unvitiated-Adamic being. No one who takes human suffering seriously takes refuge in that kind of creation theology. No one, moreover, who appreciates what the church should be craves the lost "universal-spiritual-metaphysical" background. For the church makes it clear that Christ is far more primal than pristine Adam.

With sinless Adam, one had at best the genuine "ontic I-Thou relation," particularly where Adam's relationship to God was concerned. In sinless Christ, however, and in his church, one has more than that — one has "a real connection of love between an I and an I" (SC, 40). This I-and-I does not contradict Bonhoeffer's assertion that true I-ness is discovered only in relation to alien "Thou-ness." Remember:

> The basic social category is the I-Thou relation. The Thou of the other . . . is the divine Thou. So the way to the other . . . is also the way to the divine Thou, a way of recognition or rejection. In the "moment" the individual again and again becomes a person through the "other." The other . . . presents us with the same problem of cognition as does God. . . . My real relation to the other . . . is oriented on my relation to God. But since I first know God's "I" in the revelation of . . . love, so too with the other . . . here the concept of the church finds its place. (37)

I-and-I has nothing to do with sameness, particularly given what Bonhoeffer called "a real connection of love." Love requires dissonance — so what is stressed in this I-and-I is the ineffably intimate, Christ-won and Spirit-led, agapic relation between Creator and creature. I and I: ". . . the Christian person achieves his true nature when God does not confront him as Thou, but 'enters into' him as I."

"Hence the individual belongs essentially and absolutely with the other, according to the will of God, even though, or even because, each is completely separate from the other" (37). Once again, barrier is blessing, for the integrity of the creature is intact to the extent that he or she obeys rather than vies with God. Jesus, for Bonhoeffer, is perfect in that love — hence the I-and-I — the one-of-a-kind relationship between heaven and earth.

This love between an I and an I — meaning now the church-as-Christ-existing-as-community and God — was nurtured through "a pure association of authority" — *Herrschaftsverband* — in which ruling is serving, and, serving, ruling: God, in illimitable service to humankind, "rules limitlessly." If man and woman had served God limitlessly, God would have been loved in the love — the service — one person gives to another.

In the Beginning, God's omni-rule was subtle — as if Providence were on auto-pilot. There was immediate community — "the absolute identity of purpose of the divine and human will, within the relation of the creative to the created, that is, the obedient will. In other words, within the relation of ruling and serving." As alterities were integral to such immediacy — for "all persons are created unique" — conflict within that community was unavoidable; "even in the community of love the tension between wills is not abolished" (41).

Before the fall — "the medieval symbolism for the fall puts a tree in the centre, with the serpent coiled round it, and on either side the man and the woman, separated by the tree from which they disobediently ate" — such conflict was benign because it arose from the will to serve and not from the libidinous will to self-gratification (42). One can know that, however, only in the church, which puts before one the reality of his or her sin. The "pure association of authority" — reflecting Bonhoeffer's unfortunate, because chauvinistic, views on women — is known in Christ's church alone.

Faith in Christ alone reveals "the connection between original, innate human spirituality and sociality" (43). That is, professed Bonhoeffer, God, in person, must reveal that the Christian's ontic "substance," at once spiritual and moral, is inseparable from sociality. More: God-in-the-flesh is sociality's foundation — such that "The I and the Thou are fitted into one another in infinite nearness, in mutual penetration, for ever inseparable, resting on one another, in inmost mutual participation, feeling and experiencing together, and sustaining the general stream of spiritual interaction" (48).

This "infinite nearness," "mutual penetration," is discovered in an I-and-I relationship; for "it is in the concept of the church which first makes it clear that this immediate community means something more than the ontic I-Thou relation" (40). *Something more* is discovered among Christians able to overcome their racism: Racism shackles I-Thou relationships to such an extent that only an amazing grace — an I-and-I relationship indeed — can free persons from their sameness, open them to the givenness of immediate community, in Christ.

The more an individual derives satisfaction from being a closed I, the more that individual realizes an openness to others. (Remember that Bonhoeffer could no more be *Frank* Fisher than Frank Fisher could be *Dietrich* Bonhoeffer: The undeniable *integrities* of their unique personhoods is what Bonhoeffer means by closed I's. Yet their friendship thrived in Harlem because of their openness to each other's uniqueness — an openness based on the mystery, the closedness, of the Other. In short, one has to be a healthy, as in a nonbigoted, person to see the Other as a gift, as one who is *necessary* for one's *own* — as in enclosed — well-being.)

Bonhoeffer understands this closed-ness and openness as the "collective person" — discovered only where individual persons are: "But since the collective person as a centre of acts is possible only as a concrete purposive community, it can only be possible where the individual is a real part of the concrete community" (SC, 51). Community is the essential thing. The I-Thou, so important to Bonhoeffer's life and thought, brings dissonance to mind again, for barriers are not dissolved in the collective person. And this is primarily because the collective person's vital Thou is God, "the all-embracing Person," who keeps the mystery of the Other ever before one.

God's all-embracing Person is given to the church in such a way that "collective and individual persons have the same structure, both closed and open, with mutual completion, and social and introversive intentions within a structural unity" (52). God serves, and thus rules, each person, to such an extent that all within the church stand as one (which would be impossible in a racist church: a racist church is a disobedient church). Yet, the collective person also stands as individual persons — I as well as Thou — before God. (The very concept of individuality is meaningless, however, if one is adverse to others simply on the basis of externals — skin color, hair, and so forth.) "In [God's] sight," writes Bonhoeffer, "the community and the individual are present at the same moment, and rest in one another" (52). The "monadic image of social life" is, therefore, exceeding rich (68). Communal oneness is what it is by virtue of its diversity. (Churches that mirror a racist society's mores never attain diversity on account of its sameness. Closed-ness alone prevails, to the exclusion of openness.)

That Bonhoeffer does not mean by this collectivity a "mystical fusion" is made clear by his dictum that "strife is the basic sociological law." The wills that make up the church, as a community of will, give to the church a relative content. So what the church means shifts in accordance with individual interpretations of its mission; and this involves strife — the life-nurturing struggle to promote agreement. While, as I have noted, there is, on account of the fall, "no concrete strife in the genuine sense," the strife-exacerbated-by-sin nonetheless renders sociality visible.

Even unholy contention demands a certain recognition of another; and church community, no matter how truncated, is established through some "co-operation" by dint of Providence. That is, Bonhoeffer thought that the "sinful will is forced in this struggle into the will of God, and thus community is established" (SC, 55). Without the strife that is conducive to cooperation, chaos would reign. Without the revelation, for instance, that God is not the god of racism, community would be no community to speak of. For in such a "community" (i.e., "church"), "the sin is the will to affirm in principle oneself [the Same] and not the other as a value, and to acknowledge the other only in relation to oneself" (82).

Bonhoeffer's *The Communion of Saints* examines a *legislation* of wills in a "structure of meaning" or a "structure of purpose." The *structure of purpose* is characteristic of an association that is but a means to an end. The *structure of meaning,* however, is an end in itself: "A structure of meaning is not constructed with a purpose, nor can it be explained by means of a purpose" (SC, 56). Assimilating F. Tönnies's sociology, Bonhoeffer argues that meaning is to community as purpose is to society. I find that his Harlem experience sheds light on that distinction.

When in the United States for the first time, Bonhoeffer experienced culture shock, for he was out of his society. But he felt at home, relatively speaking, in Harlem's Abyssinian Baptist Church. There he found meaning among those who — excluded for all intents and purposes from society — found solace in meeting for the sake of being together. "Betwixt and between" them, Bonhoeffer, an alien in the midst of aliens, found common "feeling, willing, and responsibility," for the "basic attitude [was] mutual inner interest" (57).

In New World society, however, where whites are over blacks, the "basic spiritual attitude is mutual inner indifference, strictest caution towards the other, leading to reserve and self-assurance [for whites primarily], and finally to a conventional amiability, so far as this consorts with [one's] purpose" (58). Society holds together in a "relation of power" — power wielded unjustly, in a way that thrives on contradictions anchored in the problem of racism. That is, to quote Bonhoeffer, "strife that had become unholy through evil" has been apparent in the ongoing mistreatment of African-Americans.

It is not that a society, itself based on community from a biblical point of view, is evil by its very nature. "But the evil will at work in a society turns it into an institution for the systematic exploitation of its members" (SC, 82). As an "organized structure of purposes," the United States itself grew from slave labor. As I assimilate Bonhoeffer, in the light of my experience as an African-American, this means that such a society — my society — is "based on contract as the origin and criterion of the association, and develops into a comprehensive system of means . . . fixed in records and agreements" (58). It is not that a "'contract' as such is . . . evil. It is only evil when it consciously exploits or destroys the other" (81-83).

The blacks Bonhoeffer fraternized with were, by and large, the descendants of slaves, the progeny of Africans, who, as chattel, were bartered in the contract arrangement. Until this very day, they have been unable to escape their domination, inherent as it has been to American capitalism as a "comprehensive system of means."

Historically, the black community has provided refuge from such a society; and the hub of this community has been the black church.

I think that Bonhoeffer, having written his dissertation on the church, found that much of his thesis came alive: At Abyssinian he discovered a community not unlike the *Herrschaftsverband.* The community was a refuge from the abuse of authority in American society. In the absence of power based on wealth, position, and caste — notwithstanding the upper class and high caste of Abyssinian's powerful pastor (but that was not power as *such*) — there was only authority of the kind that is weak in the world. That is, "there [was] presupposed an understanding of the command by the one who obeys" (SC, 58).

Presaging his argument in *The Cost of Discipleship,* Bonhoeffer found that "sociologically significant in so far as in an association of power there can be no community, whereas in one of genuine authority community is not only present, but for the most part realised. This is most important for the concept of the church" (58-59). In the black church, Bonhoeffer found persons who knew what it meant to obey, for the people had faith in the One who was to be obeyed. As one spiritual puts it,

> King Jesus rides on a milk-white horse,
> No man can a-hinder me;
> The river of Jordan he did cross,
> No man can a-hinder me . . .

Even though Ernst Feil argues that Bonhoeffer's focus on christology came well after *The Communion of Saints,* he nonetheless found at Abyssinian what he thought was a deep, and therefore structural, understanding of authority — Christ, the Savior, in whom there is a perfect association of power between God and the Saints.

One today might well argue in circles where dogmatic symbols hold sway that the church must live out its claim that there is a Holy Spirit, who gives community and "is also the principle of unity." (SC, 101). Otherwise, the manifold and toxic bigotries that reign in the world reign in the church as well. Where that occurs, too much of society is present in what should be a community that lives beyond history to God. For true community, unlike society, is, according to Bonhoeffer, transhistorical, and not teleological, insofar as it has no historic purpose that, once attained, dies.

To quote Bonhoeffer:

From all this it follows that society and community have a different view of time. In a community the intention reaches to the bounds of time, in a society it is bounded by time. This eschatological character, which a community shares with history, contains its deepest meaning, as *being given* [emphasis added] "from God to God." This is the basis of the "holiness" of human life in community, whether it is a physical community of blood and race, or a historical community like the nation, or a community of destiny like marriage or friendship. It is in virtue of this holiness that all such human structures are in principle indissoluble. The idea of society, on the other hand, does not go beyond the idea of the goal which constitutes it; it is temporal, and intra-historical. For a society the end of history is really an end, and not just a boundary. (SC, 67)

Whether it is a physical community of blood and race, or a historical community like the nation, or a community of destiny like marriage or friendship has nothing, really, to do with holiness. Holiness is the gift of life, given by God: Neither race, nor nationality, nor friendship, nor marriage is worth much unless one appropriates each through faith in God, which transcends them all.

If "wills have joined together for the sake of their joining, if a community has been affirmed, irrespective of rational purpose tendencies, then the intentionality in these acts reaches to the limits of time, i.e. to the limits of history, to God: it is 'from God to God'" (SC, 62). *To God and from God beyond the limits of history:* Community is, in reality, far more of an eschatological than a teleological phenomenon — part of what has been given us. It is by virtue of the body of Christ — flesh, blood, bone, will, soul, mind — that the community lives to God: "This is my body given for you. Do this as often as you need it in memory of me." This same Christ who serves the body, rules the body, not unlike the way God rules the body that is Jesus's own.

Almost a decade before the Nazi crisis, Dietrich Bonhoeffer realized that the will to exclude the Thou from the church could only kill the body because such a will ran counter to the church's spiritual form — love. Bonhoeffer knew that when society's mores penetrate the body of Christ, the human family itself is in peril. As I have suggested in my previous chapter, Bonhoeffer felt that acutely when his brother-in-law, his twin sister's husband, was excluded from the church because he was of Jewish descent. The marriage between his sister and her husband, however, negated the view that Jews and Aryans comprised different races — were different biologically — which throws light on Bonhoeffer's conclusion that sin and death, the upshot of racism, are ethical conundrums more so than biological phenomena analogous to the libido.

That is, the expulsion from the German church of persons of Jewish descent was not racial — in the sense of something over which one had no control. Their expulsion stemmed from a deformed (as in nazified) will — the illusion that Jew and Aryan were really different biologically — which is a continuum of the primal decision to forsake God. Jews and Aryans were different with respect to heritage, to be sure; but only to a certain, and superficial, extent. Whatever genuine difference there was, whatever alterity, was to be discovered person-to-person, I-to-Thou — which would have been a blessing. The truth, as Bonhoeffer knew early on, is that race, especially when considered eschatologically, is a collectivity that rules out the apotheosis of sameness and therefore racism. And only one who sees the absolute folly in sameness can confront the guilt, the pain, the shame, the anxiety — the sin! — he or she is bound to feel in a racialized world. For only in that way does an individual feel his or her connection to the whole human race, especially to that part vulnerable to genocide.

Bonhoeffer put it this way: "So far as we mean by 'race' the concept of the biological species, we weaken the ethical seriousness of the concept of guilt." He understood "the human species in terms of the concept of sin." Without that understanding — without the realization that race is an ethical and not a biological concept — "children, idiots [sic], and normally developed people [would] . . . all . . . be included equally." But then children as well as the mentally challenged would be expected to be as responsible as well-endowed adults. That view would lead to "a view of sin, of sacraments, and of the church, that was ethically indifferent." "So the concept of guilt must not be understood in terms of the concept of the species, but vice-versa."

> In this way we reach an ethical collective concept of the race, which is able to meet the requirements of the idea of the race's sin. The individual is then established as the self-conscious and self-active person, which is the presupposition for ethical relevance. And the race is understood as consisting of such persons. (SC, 78)

What Bonhoeffer said bears repeating.

The individual is . . . the self-conscious and self-active person, which is the presupposition for ethical relevance. And the race is understood as consisting of such persons. Whether they be Jewish, Aryan, black or white is not important. Black, white, Jew, Aryan are adjectives — epiphenomena — that are irrelevant to each I and each Thou — to the "original community of love."

The "original community of love, as the repose of wills in mutual action, is destroyed when one will exchanges the movement of love for an egocentric movement," wrote Bonhoeffer (SC, 81). Racism is precisely that egocentrism. In order to totalize the world for selfish gain — given the facts of New World slavery — the master race debases the servant race. (As the award-winning Nigerian novelist, Chinua Achebe, has put it, "If Europe, advancing in civilization, could cast a backward glance periodically at Africa trapped in primordial barbarity it could say with faith and feeling: There go I but for the grace of God. Africa is to Europe as the picture is to Dorian Gray — a caricature on to whom the master unloads his physical and moral deformities so that he may go forward, erect and immaculate" [Achebe 1989, 17].) Through faith, however, community is maintained daily, as Adam and as Christ. Through this faith, the body of Christ is empowered to struggle vigilantly against sin. The church that maintains this tension between the flesh (Adam = racism) and the Spirit (Christ = community) is one (I = I) — "even though it consists throughout of individuals; it is a collective person and yet subject to endless fragmentation; it is Adam, as every individual is both himself and Adam. This duality is its nature, annulled only by the unity of the new [humankind] in Christ" (SC, 85). This is the unity given to the communion of saints:

> Makes me love everybody . . .
> It is good when I'm in trouble . . .
> It will do when I am dying . . .

To the extent that it is an eschatological gift, what has been given is neither a religious community nor the "kingdom of God." If the church were a religious community, its personality would be confused with a proselytizing zeal that Bonhoeffer called "religious motives" — "the urge to do missionary work, the need to impart one's faith, etc." (SC, 88). A missionary's zest to convert the "heathen" (the colonized Africans, for instance) is but religious zest. A fundamentalist's confusion of faith with a subjective "holiness" (in which abstention from drinking and dancing is tantamount to spiritual discipline) is but religious confusion. In the former, a totalizing metaphysics is at work for the purposes of Western civilization. In the latter, a self-righteous ethic is put into play, for the evangelical individual often thinks himself better than the Other (for the most superficial of reasons).

The metaphysics-loving missionary exemplifies the confusion of the church with the kingdom of God. The path of Western civilization, opened by the church, was thought to be the essence of Providence, not a contingent historical process among other processes also ruled by God — destined to die. The Western church is not the kingdom of God; no church is. The church, any church, is the kingdom of Christ, according to Bonhoeffer. After all, Christians are sinners; they make up the church, and it would be presumptuous for sinners to confuse who they are in Jesus with the kingdom of God.

In distinguishing God's kingdom from Christ's, Bonhoeffer made a distinction between the communion of saints and the empirical church. The empirical church may be said to entail the local churches that make up denominations and their objective spirits. The communion of saints, however, is eminently ecumenical — it is the real world, the whole "of all the places at which the gospel is proclaimed. . . . It is one Body, real community, *sanctorum communio*" — the church where Christ and the Spirit reign in the innermost selves of I's and Thou's (SC, 154). The *communion of saints* is the kingdom of Christ, which is the kingdom of God only proleptically. Saints are therefore humble — for Christ himself calls one to ponder the irreducibility of the human and the divine. Christ, himself, has historical limits that point to humanity alone, and not to divinity, though the two are never torn asunder in him.

The kingdom of Christ pertains to those "elected in Christ." The kingdom of God, however, pertains to "all the predestined" (SC, 151). God's kingdom "exists from eternity to eternity"; Christ's kingdom "has its beginning in history." The church begins in the first century, and not really before. "In its visible historical form it comprises many more members than the kingdom of God, but in its essence not a single member more. (Rather, many members fewer . . .)" (151). The empirical church that, in atomistic fashion, mistakes itself — its objective spirit — for God's kingdom loses sight of this: God's love of the predestined before and after the church. "None," wrote Bonhoeffer, can know "whether our neighbor has been elected, or has remained impenitent. He is completely nontransparent to us in all that he does. This means not only that nothing is known about a man's *donum perseverantiae,* but also that

Christian actions can spring from a hypocritical, misguided heart, governed by a false enthusiasm" (196). It is far better to give one's neighbors — whether "Greeks, Jews, Pietists, Liberals," blacks, whites, men, women — the benefit of the doubt: The most important thing is to live out the faith that God is no respecter of persons.

Faith, Bonhoeffer thought, is thus far deeper than "human fellow-feeling" that despises dissonance and seeks to level community because there is not between I and Thou "the true fire of Christ" (SC, 170). Bigotry lurks beneath such disingenuousness, which is why Bonhoeffer wrote:

> Is not the profession of the church and of brotherly love at its most unequivocal precisely when there are such complete safeguards against its being confused in any way with any kind of human fellow-feeling? Does not this kind of communion [i.e., love, the antithesis of human fellow-feeling] in which Jew remains Jew, Greek Greek, worker worker and capitalist capitalist, and yet all are the Body of Christ, much better preserve the reality of the *sanctorum communio* than the one in which the hard fact of human differences is veiled in deceptive mildness? (170)

Indeed, the failure to embrace alterity with candor as well as love produces a human fellow-feeling that is but thinly disguised sameness. Such sameness illustrates Bonhoeffer's contention that the empirical church carries within it "two fundamental tendencies warring against each other, and both are destined to flourish in a constant increase of violence and power." These two for Bonhoeffer were "the *sanctorum communio* and the *Antichrist*." Within the empirical church Bonhoeffer represented the faithful, "the striving of the *sanctorum communio* to penetrate all human life, whether community or society" (SC, 199).

Surely, devotees of the Antichrist embodied a xenophobic (objective) spirit — a phony "human fellow-feeling" — a quasi incestuousness that so misunderstood the kingdom of Christ that it tried to wrest the Last Judgment from God. And surely, those possessed

71

by the Antichrist — the "One" akin to the nothingness Karl Barth calls antisoteriological — assumed that people such as the Jews and the Africans had no place in "heaven."

Bonhoeffer held that a saint-in-communion-with-others always had in view those "two fundamental tendencies warring against each other, but with an understanding of "the inner necessity of the idea of apocatastasis." Who knows who is sure to go to "heaven"? Bonhoeffer has reminded us that "we are not in a position to resolve this antimony." For: "In the concept of the church, as the presence of Christ in the world urging us to a decision, the double issue is just as necessarily required as it appears impossible to us, perceiving that we in no way merit the gift of God's undeserved love we have received, that others should be excluded from this gift and this love" (SC, 201). "It will not do to be too hasty to rub out the antinomy," writes one African theologian. "How Jesus gathers up all things in himself will be manifest only on the 'last day.' Meanwhile there is life's polyphony, and it may not be refused" (Boulaga 1984, 188). The Last Day is ever before us. *It's good enough for me. . . . It will take us* all *to heaven.*

II
Act and Being

How does one appropriate this "old time religion" that transcends itself in its eschatological reality, but is open to sociological analysis? How does one who would be a saint live as a saint — love the Thou, transcend the limitations of the "empirical church"? Bonhoeffer's *Act and Being* provides a few answers.

He argues that being encompasses prereflective consciousness as well as reflective consciousness. In its prereflective mode, consciousness is drawn to someone spontaneously — turns to her as it were; and this immediate turning may be said to be an act — the reference to, the intentionality toward, what is other than the self. Even though consciousness and act operate closely together in this, Bonhoeffer makes it clear that consciousness is closer to being than to act. In his own words:

72

The juxtaposition of act and being is not identical with that of consciousness and being, for the latter pair of concepts is not mutually exclusive in its terms. Even consciousness has predicates of being, for as conscious-*ness* it embodies the ontological category of the conscious. The act, inasmuch as it is pure intentionality, must be considered wholly alien to being. That it is consciously executed necessitates the distinction between direct *(actus directus)* and reflexive *(actus reflexus)* consciousness: in the first, conscious-ness is simply "directed at"; in the second, it can become objec-tively conscious of itself in reflexion. It is not, then, that the act offers no *material* to reflexion, only that the intentionality of the direct act is automatically displaced by reflexion — in relation to which, therefore, it cannot stand as a datum that was "there" for the finding. (AB, 12-13)

So while being is appropriated through the givenness of conscious-ness, act *must be considered wholly alien to being.* Bonhoeffer is clear about this distinction, for the cart does not pull the horse. Being comes first. Only after we are here, on this earth, do *we* have cause to respond to something or someone, and to make use of hindsight. The *actus directus,* which Bonhoeffer himself calls *direct* conscious-ness, is that initial response (by way of one's inward eye, one might say).

(Heuristically, in my mind's eye, I think of a primordial being, a long-ago ancestor, who has only recently begun to walk upright. Striking an old tree, setting it aflame, a flash of red hot lightening startles him. The ancestor is riveted by what he sees, for he had not seen the awesomeness of nature's spontaneous combustion. He is *directed by* what he sees, and so cannot help but *direct* his attention *to* it. Direct consciousness has both of those implications as I see it — being made to see and intending to see. *How can this be!* wonders the ancestor, for he is not in control of the situation.)

There is no self-sufficiency in *actus directus:* "Only when exis-tence, supposed in permanent orientation to transcendence, is said not to be able to understand itself (or only to understand that it does

73

not understand itself) is the true sense of *the act* expressed." Contingent being is thus the basis of self-transcendence — one's recognition of the world's continuity and otherness. The immediacy of that primal recognition is unpredictable (for, to modify Bonhoeffer's language, the act is an ever-shifting-with-reference-to). One must understand too that act is "utter intentionality" — "something which gives proof of itself in the psychic process but is only to be understood on the far side of it, act as 'direct' consciousness — *actus directus*" (AB, 28).

Not unlike the way one is riveted to the spirited music created at the spur of the moment in jazz improvisation — yet must be content with only the memory of the startling experience — the *actus directus* dissipates after the occasion is over. One, in reflecting upon the occasion during which such immediacy was experienced, is faced with the absence of that event itself. To reiterate Bonhoeffer's point: *The direct act is automatically displaced by reflexion — in relation to which, therefore, it cannot stand as a datum that was "there" for the finding.* Flanked by the limiting enigmas of life and death, the self knows its moment of direct consciousness as truly short-lived.

And we are brought back to the question: How does one appropriate this "old time religion" that is both eschatological and sociological? How does one live as a saint, love the Thou, transcend the limitations of the "empirical church"?

Whether one lives the saintly life, loves the Thou, and transcends the limitations of the empirical church has everything to do with whether one understands the barrier between act and being. For act entails how we relate to others and how we relate, therefore, to God — how open we are to the wide scope of being that has been given us. Far more important than reflection on consciousness is the direct consciousness of the Other; for that *actus directus* will bear on how one lives: How did one look at this Other in the first place; what was arresting about this Other?

The issue is all the more critical when act abuses being in racist intentions. One sees clearly then the significance of Bonhoeffer's view that "the meaning of epistemology is anthropology" (AB, 14).

When one's inward eye has gazed on the Other and abused her for the sake of the bluest eye (remember this talk about the bluest eye from my Preface), knowledge, as anthropology, is truncated. Can one enjoy human being fully if the epistemologies that deign to define humankind stem from exceedingly narrow acts?

With the racist, such narrowness means that the arresting thing that makes its way into reflection is the lack of sameness. (Remember this from the introduction: *The first difference that strikes us is that of color.*) As Winthrop Jordan explains in his *White over Black: American Attitudes Toward the Negro, 1550-1812,* the Anglo-Saxons looked on the Africans as the antithesis of themselves. "The impact of the Negro's color was the more powerful upon Englishmen . . . because England's principal contact with Africans came in West Africa and the Congo where men were not merely dark but almost literally black: one of the fairest-skin nations suddenly came face to face with one of the darkest people on earth" (Jordan 1977, 6). "From the first," then,

> Englishmen tended to set Negroes over against themselves, to stress what they conceived to be radically contrasting qualities of color, religion, and style of life, as well as animality and a peculiarly potent sexuality. What Englishmen did not at first fully realize was that Negroes were potentially subjects for a special kind of obedience and subordination which was to arise as adventurous Englishmen sought to possess for themselves and their children one of the most bountiful dominions of the earth. (Jordan 1977, 43)

In other words, the upshot of that *actus directus* was the metaphysical, because illusory, view that blacks were both ugly and inferior and deserved to be enslaved in order to make the New World yield its bounty. This *actus reflexus* legitimized slavery; for the whites had not "left behind all the impressions initially gathered of the *Negro* before he became preeminently the *slave*" (Jordan 1977).

As was the case with *The Communion of Saints,* I find that *Act and Being* makes it imperative for one to understand the difference between such metaphysics, tied as it is to European philosophy, and

Bonhoeffer's Christian philosophy. European philosophy has legitimized, in fact, the racist attitudes Jordan explores in *White over Black*. For, as Cornel West brings out in his *Prophecy Deliverance,* Hume and Kant had looked on the Africans racist-ly (West 1982, 62). That fact makes Bonhoeffer's revisiting of Germany's great philosophers in *Act and Being* fascinating, though he examined them primarily in order to expose the chimera, the fantasy, of human consciousness in which God is but a hypothesis.

The Enlightened mind, *à la* Kant, held that the knowing I was part of a cosmos that existed, it appeared, so that matter might conform to thought — a view emergent from the transcendence of a world ordered by the knowing subject. Bonhoeffer, however, held that there was no real transcendence in Kant. As Bonhoeffer saw it, the philosopher's self-understanding, glorified as reason, was too subjective. For Bonhoeffer, then, "Philosophy, thought, the I, are forfeit to themselves instead of to the transcendental" (AB, 25). The world itself is therefore a projection of the self. One might say the alienated self's logos and mettle is but a projection of erudite, European consciousness upon the world's alterity.

Remember: Kant was hardly progressive in his views on the so-called Negro. He wrote in his *Observations on the Feeling of the Beautiful and Sublime:*

> Mr. Hume challenges anyone to cite a simple example in which a negro has shown talents, and asserts that among the hundreds of thousands of blacks who are transported elsewhere from their countries, although many of them have been set free, still not a single one was ever found who presented anything great in art and science or any other praiseworthy quality, even though among the whites some continually rise aloft from the lowest rabble, and through superior gifts earn respect in the world. So fundamental is the difference between the two races of man, and it appears to be as great in regard to mental capacities as in color. (cited in West 1982, 62-63)

That *actus reflexus* forgot that its direct act was to itself, in the sense that it labored under the illusion of self-sufficiency — to such an extent that God was but a possibility; tenable, for Kant, only in terms of an impossible self-motivated appeal to ethical purity.

But such an arrogant assumption — that human beings could live out the Golden Rule as a Maxim — is but "ontic narcissism" for Bonhoeffer. Such narcissism also typifies Hegelian idealism, which is "neighbor to materialism, Hegel to Marx"; and so, as is the case with Kantian transcendentalism, a certain atheism is at work. The ultimate is man — whether one means by that the absolute Spirit en route to itself, or the classless, stateless society. So "whence could come any self-understanding from outside the self if the I is the creator of the world" (AB, 26-27)?

This encapsulated I, who thinks himself creator, is seen, I think, in the very cavalier way Hegel has cast aspersion on the African people in his *Philosophy of History:* "The Negro . . . exhibits the natural man in his completely wild and untamed state. *We* [emphasis added] must lay aside all thought of reverence and morality — all that we call feeling — if we would rightly comprehend him; there is nothing harmonious with humanity to be found in this type of character" (Hegel 1956, 93). I also think that Hegel's racism supports Bonhoeffer's claim: "It simply is not true that concrete man (including even the philosopher) is in full possession of the mind. Whoever countenances the idea that he need only arrive at himself to be in God is doomed to hideous disillusion in experiencing the utter introversion, the treadmill confinement to the self, of the loneliest solitude, with its tormenting desolation and sterility" (AB, 28). *Cor curvum in se.*

Hegel, Bonhoeffer has implied, played God, and this is why the idealist mind is lost — it has foundered "on the resistance of [its] own reality" (AB, 27). According to Bonhoeffer, Hegelian hubris is "an illusion of movement within a self-contained repose" (38). God is found in self-aggrandizement: "Hegel wrote a philosophy of angels, but not of human existence" (27). This godliness — a Promethean pride — is at the root of theories of racial supremacy. V. Y.

Mudimbe brings out clearly the ethical insufficiency of such a view as he places it in larger historical context:

> The problem is that during this period [of Enlightenment] both imperialism and anthropology took shape, allowing the reification of the "primitive." The key is the idea of History with a capital H, which first incorporates St. Augustine's notion of *providentia* and later on expresses itself in the evidence of Social Darwinism. Evolution, conquest, and difference become signs of a theological [i.e., religious], biological, and anthropological destiny, and assign to things and beings both their natural slots and social mission. Theorists of capitalism . . . as well as philosophers, comment upon two main and complementary paradigms. These are the inherent superiority of the white race, and, as already made explicit in Hegel's *Philosophy of Right,* the necessity for European economies and structures to expand to "virgin areas" of the world. (Mudimbe 1988, 17)

What better than that exemplifies what Bonhoeffer meant by *ontic narcissism?* Bonhoeffer recognized that it was one thing to wrestle with the heart-stopping *angst* born from contingency — "the outrage, which [human beings feel] at 'being already' 'with reference to' some other thing which transcends [them]" (AB, 28). Far better — and Freud's *Future of an Illusion* comes to mind here — to assuage the keen anxiety through collapsing the Absolute into the *angst*-ridden self. But it is something else again to storm the Other — the African Other in this case — with the "starting-point of the I" (the imperious bluest eye). Bonhoeffer's point here (as I, an African-American, assimilate his German Thou) is that the atheism in idealism is seen not so much in what the philosopher thinks, as in what the ethical implications of his view are likely to be.

These ethical implications are all the more critical given the claim that idealism, as alienated *actus directus* and alienated *actus reflexus,* has made its way into Christianity. This means that a Christian philosophy that is but a warmed-over idealism has never had its consciousness directed to God-in-Christ. Bonhoeffer put it this way: "The gospel of mind finding itself in God and God in itself was preached too seductively by idealism for theology to resist its blandishments, and all too readily it reasoned thus: if being is essentially consciousness, God must 'be' in religious experiences, and the re-born I must find God in reflexion on itself" (AB, 38-39). Bonhoeffer has just described a "Christian" atheism, oxymoron though it may be, that would totalize the world.

But not one bit of the world God has made is fit to be colonized, for not a bit of the world can be mastered by men — the dissonance of I and Thou has not permitted it (not totally). Those who would colonize a people, with the rationale of some enlightened epistemology or the other, fail to see that their desire to totalize, as in civilize, others stems from a failure to understand who they are. Can they master the world when they cannot master themselves?

That they cannot is given in the very structure of the *actus directus* itself. Direct consciousness never masters the being that gives rise to it: What the conscious mind "looks on" directly cannot, in fact, *stand as a datum that was "there" for the finding,* as if the self were the cosmos' limit and not limited by the cosmos. For the sake of community, the direct act, in refusing to "turn the I into the Creator," must arise with respect to the barrier (AB, 30).

According to Bonhoeffer "God's non-objectivity [is] behind the activity of consciousness," such that "the existentially God-intending act takes place in the *actus directus* but is inaccessible to the reflexion of consciousness on itself" (AB, 38). This means that only one who recognizes that God, and concomitantly other people, cannot be domesticated is faithful to "the contingent action of God on [the human race]" (47). Without that recognition, human consciousness would remain, unwittingly, an enigma to itself, for it would never gain clarity as to the scope of being, which is gained from the Other — who has been given us.

Genuine theology reflects on this givenness and thus occurs within "the reference of revelation to the consciousness," appropriating that consciousness "as act" (AB, 48). Graced with revelation, theology affirms "being transcendent of consciousness" in terms of a redemptive ontology that sees "the continuity of [humankind] and revelation" (AB, 108). One wants to know: what is this field, this numinous milieu, which — despite the reality of death — is so life-giving, and — ineffable?

Grace alone answers that question: It was Bonhoeffer's contention that we have before us, always, a sure sense of what has been given us — Christ, concretely, in act and in being. Christ, himself, is life-giving and (à la *actus directus*) ineffable. In Christ, God looks on us, turns toward us (act), giving us the divine Thou (being).

Yes, the quintessential Act and Being are God's, for "God's being is solely act." If one has a true ontology, which means that one has first and foremost a true theology, one would know "God's being is solely act," because God would have called one — one would have looked to Christ — directly. If I "am still reflecting on myself in order to find Christ, Christ is not there. If he is really there, I *see* [added] only him" (AB, 161).

So much is this an injunction against self-deification that one might well agree with Barth that the finite cannot contain the infinite *(finitum incapax infiniti)*. Bonhoeffer, however, found God's Being far too real to be given over to the Last Day. It was thus important for Bonhoeffer to say: "In revelation it is a question less of God's freedom on the far side from us, i.e. his eternal isolation and aseity, than of his forth-proceeding, his *given* Word, his bond in which he has bound himself, of his freedom as it is most strongly attested in his having freely bound himself to historical man, having placed himself at man's disposal" (AB, 90). God's accessibility, then, does not retreat into the modalistic inscrutability of the essential being. God is "not in eternal non-objectivity," but God is here, "'haveable,' graspable in [the] Word within the Church" (91). (It is in that sense that Bonhoeffer is true to his Lutheran heritage, as opposed to Calvin's legacy in Barth. In fact, Bonhoeffer quotes Luther in a footnote, making the point that God in Christ is eminently haveable: "It is the honor and glory of our God . . . that, giving himself for our sake in deepest condescension, he passes into the flesh, the bread, our hearts, mouths, entrails, and suffers also for our sake that he be dishonorably handled, on the altar as on the cross" [AB, 81].)

God is there in faith — *the precondition of which is revelation*. One knows then that being is a gift: It comes from outside of the self; it precedes consciousness, whether construed as *actus directus* or *actus reflexus*. Revelation is not in that sense transcendent act merely, for "God 'is' in it." And since God is in it, given to us in revelation, one realizes that his or her being is prior to the *actus directus* — that one has been created — "and acts only out of that 'being.'" This being, grace, is objective, to be sure, and thus transcends consciousness. But, "it can somehow be brought to givenness, it exists, is there, present, accessible, in being; it is independent of the consciousness, does not fall into its power" (AB, 108).

"From this it follows that when revelation is understood *only* as doctrine, the Christian idea of revelation eludes the grasp, because there has been an attempt to seize God with an ontological apparatus . . . adequate only to the human" (109). Doctrine is inadequate because what occurs in the depth of one's being is more pertinent to faith than to doctrine. Far more important than what one thinks doctrinally is what has been given him and why.

As I noted in my discussion of Bonhoeffer's rejection of the German Christians, both the racist Christian and the one who finds racism abhorrent may agree on the indispensability of "a doctrine of the merciful God, even one which states that wherever man and God come together, there the Cross must stand." The *theologia crucis* "is in itself no stumbling-block" but could well be "a welcome addition to our 'system.'" What our system is, however — meaning what our doctrine is — depends, writes Bonhoeffer, on whether "our existence is really affected," whether "we not only hear of the Cross and judgement but . . . deliver ourselves to them, that grace may descend" (AB, 109).

Therein lies the scandal as well as the stumbling-block: Whether a systematic theology gives lip service to the cross and to judgment, or whether that theology follows an irresistible call to seek freedom — because of the cross and because of judgment — is determined by whether the theologian has seen Jesus. All depends on whether there has been an *actus directus* in reference to God's Thou, and, in turn, to the Thou of the neighbor — his or her "race" notwithstanding. Only then — because of "a divinely created faith" — would there be the communion of I and I, as well as act and being, and only then would doctrine reflect on being beyond "human fellow-feeling."

To put this another way: Unless revelation pulls theology from racist intentions — "unless Christ in person speaks to us in his Word of new creation to transform our existence, unless the general proposition becomes a living occurrence" — theologians may serve Satan and not Christ (AB, 146). To serve Satan is to think that God is but an entity that serves a racist ideal, which is an all-too-subjective view in that it fails to encounter the living God, who is given despite racist living. God is not an entity, a thing that may be manipulated for partisan purposes. God is a living Thou, a living I, present where I's genuinely encounter Thou's in genuine community. It is precisely in that sense that "the revelation preached to us of God in Christ, the three-in-one person self-bestowed on us, would be the object of our knowing" (114).

A nonracist person could well consider this faith (the givenness of *the revelation preached to us of God in Christ*), in terms of the *actus reflexus* — the entity — of certain elements of the slave religion, which gave birth to the spiritual "Old Time Religion," and which hovered ghostlike at the Abyssinian Baptist Church Bonhoeffer frequented. While slave religion was not Christian in its totality, Bonhoeffer's *Act and Being* lends itself to a consideration of elements of slave religion as "faith-wishfulness," which is a form of the *actus reflexus:*

> As concrete being-assailed by Christ, the movement of faith passes in time, though not ascertainably in demonstrable theres and thens. Where and when I believed is known only to God and is

inaccessible to my reflexion. Faith abides in itself as *actus direc-tus*. . . . Nothing could be more mistaken than to deny, from the fact that everything is accessible to reflexion only *in* reflexion — therefore faith only as "faith-wishfulness" *(Gläubigkeit)*, "religios-ity" — that there is an *actus directus* taking place in time. For such a dismissal reflexion has no justification. Reflexion discovers itself always to be already in reflexion, and this very reflexion must indicate that connection to the direct act has been interrupted. This is the fundamental problem of every-dayness . . . and we are left with the condition of predicatory and theological knowledge. (AB, 141-42)

Bonhoeffer has said *that* everything *is accessible to reflexion only in reflexion — therefore faith only as* "faith-wishfulness." There is, therefore, something religious about our theologies. And that keeps the faithful humble, on the move, *leaning on the Lord.* For there was an encounter — however ineffable now — between God and the believer; and that is the foundation of all we say and do in relation to God.

Why not say that *actus directus,* taking place in time, is bound up with the memory of slavery, which is still one of the bitterest of racist legacies? What better way to assimilate Bonhoeffer's sense of com-munity — which means in *Act and Being* that "theological thought and knowledge are only possible as *ecclesiastical* thought and knowl-edge" — than in terms of the memory of the black people among whom he found a *church* home (AB, 144)? If, moreover, the person, in this case Bonhoeffer, "as a synthesis of act and being, is always two in one: *individual* and *humanity*"; if "the concept of the absolute individual is an abstraction with no corresponding reality," how better to see this than in terms of Bonhoeffer's sojourn in the black church (130)? How better to appreciate this twoness-in-oneness, this individual-and-humanity, than by way of the faith Bonhoeffer felt he had in common with the descendants of slaves?

Given the view that the reflective act, *actus reflexus,* involves a "religious" dimension — which is to be overcome, to be sure — and given the fact of the problem of racism, would it not be unwise to bracket slave religion, as if it were unfit for a consideration of the fact *that there is an* actus directus *taking place in time?* Unwise it would be: Slave religion allows us to widen our understanding of the world in seeing that the *actus reflexus* "requires a constant plunging back into the shadow of the past where time hovers ghostlike" (Ellison 1972, xix). True, the past was but background, for Bonhoeffer; unless the good news of resurrection "'coming to' us in the future should raise it to 'presence'" (AB, 119). When proclaimed, this good news carries with it the realization that no true believers are lost to the essential church, the communion of saints, for the resurrection — and the apocatastasis it implies — is what is promised. "Of the Christian revelation," as Bonhoeffer had it, "it may be said that the annunciation of Cross and resurrection, determined by eschatology and predestination, together with the event effective within it, serves even to raise the past to the present and, paradoxically, to something future yet 'to come'" (120).

It is in that forward-looking sense of what is to come — "neither slave nor free . . ." — that I refer to this Bonhoefferian faith that embracing "both entity and non-entity," living and dead, fills human beings until our actions accord with the faith that is given. By way of the faith that no event in which Christ is encountered is lost, we remember, however dimly, that we have been called to honor the Other without respect to black or white, slave or free. Notwithstanding that African-American slaves' consciousness was mediated, in significant instances, by an objective spirit derived from the continuum of African values, as opposed to European values, those slaves surely illustrate many of Bonhoeffer's points in *Act and Being.* The reality of their slave contingency, given the terrifying reality of a lifetime of radically domesticated being, was such that they had no illusion of finding God there in their truncated existence "ready-to-hand," or immanent within them, or out of reach for all intents and purposes.

To the extent that some of them really encountered the cross and its promise of resurrection — to the extent Bonhoeffer's views may be said to be true — might it not be so that they knew God as the Other;

who, while concrete in their suffering on the model of the gospel itself, was surely more than and prior to that suffering, which was nearly synonymous with being? Can one not say — despite the fact that their being was, ostensibly, limited by their master's racist acts, "the faith expressed in their spirituals indicates that some of them had seen, and really seen, Jesus in the concreteness of their suffering" — *that there was an* actus directus *taking place in time*? Is it implausible that they realized their closeness to him, in whom no one has been, or will be, really, a slave? Would not the sign of that reality be the cross, through which not a few came to know that God's Thou is inseparable from a crucified being that will level enslaving walls?

Bonhoeffer held that such faith was alive in the Abyssinian Baptist Church. And it is no wonder that the church moved him; for there were persons who could appreciate his sense of having to think about the One who is freeing and mighty — a Thou who startles and quickens in advance of the *actus reflexus*.

Slavers, Nazis, racists of every conceivable ilk, Bonhoeffer held, diminish life, in their narrow senses of who is fit and who is not. Christians, however, given the supralapsarian implications of Bonhoeffer's claim that Jesus Christ is "the new humanity itself," celebrate life, together. Being in Christ, as *sanctorum communio,* was for Bonhoeffer the totality of humankind, in proleptic realization. "For only through persons, and only through the person of Christ can [our] . . . existence . . . be affected, placed into truth and transplanted into a new manner of existing" (AB, 124). Faith and communion, then, form a unity as act and being.

Because God is the One in whom community, as being, is grounded, being is prior to act (much in the same way that grace is prior to faith). To reverse this order is antiprovidential, antisoteriological, for such reversion stems from the fallen I and is — as Bonhoeffer knew before he came face to face with the Nazis — but sin and death. "Death," wrote Bonhoeffer, "is the very source of all [the fallen I's] knowledge and volition, for they do not come from the life of God" (AB, 167). Nothing, it seems to me, verifies his point more than Germany's extermination camps — the *Vernichtungslager* — and America's lynching posts.

When Christ, argues Bonhoeffer — as I assimilate his legacy, the memory of his Thou — is the Thou of the *actus directus,* the non-being of such racist acts is replaced with the being of community, for one sees "only Christ, as . . . Lord and . . . God." And that means we see "in one and the same act, the risen and crucified *in* [our] neighbor and in creation" (181). This old-time religion, *The Communion of Saints* and *Act and Being* as faith-wishfulness — "All praying, all searching for God in [God's] Word, all clinging to [God's] promise, all entreaty for . . . grace, all hoping in sight of the Cross, all this for reflexion is 'religion,' 'faith-wishfulness'" — was good enough for Bonhoeffer. It helped him love *everybody,* as far as he could — for "in the communion of Christ, while it is still the work of man, it is God-given faith, faith willed by God, wherein by God's mercy [God-in-Christ] may really be found" (176).

> Give me that old time religion,
>   it's good enough for me . . .
> It was good for Paul and Silas . . .
> Makes me love everybody . . .
> It is good when I'm in trouble . . .
> It will do when I am dying . . .
> It will take us all to heaven . . .

Make no mistake: *The Communion of Saints* and *Act and Being* prepared Bonhoeffer well for what he would do in Harlem and against the Nazis.

These next two chapters, "Poor Pilgrims of Sorrow" and "I'm Going to Lay Down This Heavy Load," explore in added detail the significance of what Bonhoeffer did because of what had been given him — a gift he, a talented Christian intellectual, sought to understand in his early theology.

CHAPTER 3

Poor Pilgrims of Sorrow: African-Americans and Dietrich Bonhoeffer

I am a poor pilgrim of sorrow.
I'm tossed in this wide world alone.
No hope have I for tomorrow.
I've started to make heaven my home.

Sometimes I am tossed and driven.
Sometimes I don't know where to roam.
I've heard of a city called heaven,
I've started to make it my home.

That Bonhoeffer tried to love *everybody,* inasmuch as he tried to love Christ as best he could, lends great credibility to his early scholarship focused on I and Thou; act and being. And, as I have been arguing all along, what gives more credibility to his witness than his scholarship *(actus reflexus)* was his hands-on experience *(actus directus)* with *African*-Americans.

My emphasis on *African* is to make the point that Bonhoeffer encountered more than the "Negro," a peculiarly *American* creation.

He encountered a people with roots in Africa. Each time Bonhoeffer frequented Harlem, and each time he listened to the spirituals, or played them on the piano, he encountered the continuum of those roots. For they are in the faces of these black people, and in their folkways, vernacular, literature, and music — in the spirituals particularly.

I am a poor pilgrim of sorrow is from the spiritual "City Called Heaven." It is a mournful melody — griefstricken really — which is why the African-American scholar W. E. B. Du Bois, editor of the NAACP's *Crisis* when Bonhoeffer read it in 1930-1931, called the spirituals "sorrow songs." "They are the music of an unhappy people," wrote Du Bois, "the children of disappointment; they tell of death and suffering and unvoiced longing toward a truer world, of misty wanderings and hidden ways" (Du Bois 1969, 267). These *hidden ways* hark back to Africa, truthfully; for "the music is far more ancient than the words."

Witness Du Bois's memory of his great great-grandmother: ". . . my grandfather's grandmother was seized by an evil Dutch trader two centuries ago; and coming to the valleys of the Hudson and Housatonic, black, little, and lithe, she shivered and shrank in the harsh north winds, looked longingly at the hills, and often crooned a . . . melody to the child between her knees. . . . *Do bana coba, gene me, gene me!*" (1969, 267-68). The "voice of exile": *Sometimes I am tossed and driven/Sometimes I don't know where to roam.*

The implications of Bonhoeffer's relationship to these often bewildered people are given voice in his early theology, offering much in regard to the struggle against racism. Having already discussed his early theology in the light of the problem of racism, I now further explore the implications of his theology in terms of the problem of black otherness — with a focus on the theme "the African-beneath-the-Negro" and the novels *Uncle Tom's Cabin, Heart of Darkness,* and *The African.* I will also draw out the implications of this theme, the African-beneath-the-Negro, in terms of Bonhoeffer's Harlem experience — with attention to the legacy of Adam Clayton Powell

Sr. and the novel *Autobiography of an Ex-Colored Man*. Finally, I will sum up my arguments in terms of Bonhoeffer's view of Martin Luther's *Bondage of the Will* — a view related to his critique of white American theology and involvement in the life of an African-American church.

I have adopted this approach in the absence of much material regarding Bonhoeffer's sojourn in Harlem. Frank Fisher left no record of his friendship with Bonhoeffer, and virtually nothing substantial has been written on Bonhoeffer and African-Americans. Anyway, the presence of more information would not have changed what I have to say. For it is not a blow-by-blow account of what Bonhoeffer did in Harlem that concerns me. Rather, it is, indeed, the undisputed fact that Harlem and African-Americans engaged him in such a way as to challenge one to appropriate his legacy in regard to the alienness of the Other. Which is why I hit upon the theme of the African-beneath-the-Negro: nothing in the United States exposes the problem of otherness — the problem of racism — more so than this African ancestry and the Negro that was pillaged from it. The novels I have selected raise that to the level of truth: They bear on the reality of black otherness that I want to discuss in the light of Bonhoeffer's theology and witness in Harlem. In using these novels, in addition, I have had in mind Bonhoeffer's prison experience. While in jail he read novels and dabbled in the writing of literature himself — poems and short stories. I think it fair to say that Bonhoeffer would agree that novels, particularly those that attain the level of art, capture reality in ways that complement the theologian's desire to speak the truth in language that approximates faith in a timeless God.

I
Bonhoeffer and the Problem of Black Otherness

Bonhoeffer was aware of the problem of black otherness early on, it seems: Mary Bosanquet's *The Life and Death of Dietrich Bonhoeffer* reveals that the preadolescent Bonhoeffer "read a few books repeatedly, until he knew them almost by heart." One of these was "a translation of *Uncle Tom's Cabin*" — that historic novel that caused a sensation in antebellum America because it was thought to be a shocking exposé of slavery (Bonsanquet 1968, 31). Yet the novel does not reflect an understanding of the genuine alterity that Bonhoeffer discusses in *The Communion of Saints:*

> I and Thou are not just interchangeable concepts, but they comprise specifically *different* contents of experience. I myself can become the object of experience for myself, but I can never experience my own self as a Thou. . . . I can never become a real barrier for myself, but it is equally impossible for me to leap over the barrier to the *other.* (SC, 33, emphases added)

Stowe leaps *over the barrier:* The slaves who actually reveal slavery's wretchedness, George and Eliza, are really white. Two of the novel's most central characters, quadroons, who pass for *white,* they are the slaves who most eloquently bring out the horror of slavery. They are most industrious in challenging the slave regime — so industrious that they make their way to Canada where they live as *whites.*

The slaves closest to Africa — meaning those who conform to the racialist phenotype, *"Negroid"* — have little heroism about them (which says more about Stowe than the Africans). Their archetype is the inordinately pious Uncle Tom — who dies in slavery. "He was a large, broad-chested, powerfully made man, of a full glossy black, and a face whose truly African features were characterized by an expression of grave and steady good sense, united with much kindliness and benevolence" (Stowe 1981, 32). He had, according to Stowe, "the soft, impressible nature of his kindly race, ever yearning toward the simple and childlike" (162).

Uncle Tom is both the essence of the New World Negro and the personification of Stowe's African — one doomed to respond with the "invariable 'Yes, Mas'r,' for ages the watchword of poor Africa"

(Stowe 1981, 136). If Bonhoeffer is correct in his view that "in the sphere of moral reality the Thou-form is fundamentally different from the I-form"; if it is so that "the Thou, as a form which has *reality,* is *independent* in principle, over against the I in this sphere," then Stowe's Uncle Tom is bereft of Thouness (otherness) (SC, 33; emphases added).

In retrospect, though, *Uncle Tom's Cabin* may have been a fitting way to introduce young Bonhoeffer to the problem he would encounter in his late twenties. As has been brought out by the literary critic, John W. Ward, the novel focuses on slavery as the true measure of what is wrong with society, "a society breaking up into discrete, atomistic individuals where human beings, white or black, can find no secure relation one with another" (Ward 1981, 485). Bonhoeffer the young man might have well agreed with Ward's sense of the main point of the novel — "that the hard, aggressive, masterful, Anglo-Saxon ruling class is doomed in the sight of God, that America has fallen away from . . . God and that the 'signs of the times' are that a great convulsion is about to render history" (493).

A convulsion provoked by a hatred that strikes at the very foundation of America: Despite its troublesome, as in Victorian, racism, Stowe's preface makes this clear: *Uncle Tom's Cabin* has to do with "an exotic race, whose ancestors, born beneath a tropic sun, brought with them, and perpetuated to their descendants a character so essentially unlike the hard and dominant Anglo-Saxon race, as for many years to have won from it only misunderstanding and contempt."

Bonhoeffer himself realized the reality of this alien Africanness, this genuine otherness — this problem — always beneath the "Negroes" he fraternized with as Thou's to his German I in Harlem. For he wrote:

At the time of the arrival of the first large shipments of Negroes in America, who had been plundered as slaves from Africa, there was a general rejection of the idea of making the Negro Christian, particularly by the white slave-owners. Slavery was justified on the ground that the Negro was heathen. Baptism would put in question the permissibility of slavery and would bring the Negro undesirable rights and privileges. Only after a dreadful letter of reassurance from the Bishop of London, in which he promised the white masters that the external conditions of the Negro need not be altered in the least by Baptism, that Baptism was a liberation from sin and evil desire and not from slavery or from any other external fetters, did the slave owners find themselves ready to afford the Gospel an entry among the Negroes. Finally it was even found to have the advantage of keeping the slaves more easily under supervision than if they were left to continue their own pagan cults. So it came about that the Negroes became Christians and were admitted to the gallery at white services and as the last guest to the communion table. (NRS, 108)

Bonhoeffer notes that the Africans, who had been *plundered* in order to be enslaved, were denied baptism at first and had been enslaved on the ground that *the Negro was heathen*. Both of those points call for further emphasis.

The refusal to baptize Africans stemmed as much from greed as from anything else — it was particularly *the white slave-owners* who would not Christianize their chattel, lest they be seen as human beings and not beasts of burden; lest the nascent plantocracy be stripped of its material base. That baptism was later *found to have the advantage of keeping the slaves more easily under supervision than if they were left to continue their own pagan cults* brings out this insight from Bonhoeffer's early theology: The Christianity that baptized blacks, but sanctioned slavery, was not a Christianity born from an *actus directus* stayed on Christ and neighbor. Slave-holding Christianity was but a form of self-justifying religion.

With respect to the point that *Slavery was justified on the ground that the Negro was* heathen — *heathen* stripped the Africans of their humanity. *Heathen,* rejected the concrete Thou — the Africans' alterity — and tended to make slavers blind to the heathenism of another sort; namely the one that plunders and enslaves. The Africans were seen only as "strings of dusty niggers with splay feet." Better yet — to see them as "a lot of mysterious niggers" (Conrad 1970, 81, 82).

The quoted words — *strings of dusty niggers with splay feet; a lot of mysterious niggers* — are taken from Joseph Conrad's *Heart of Darkness,* a paragon of that illusory otherness produced by the metaphysician's racism. As Chinua Achebe put it: *"Heart of Darkness* projects the image of Africa as 'the other world,' the antithesis of Europe and therefore of civilization, a place where man's vaunted intelligence and refinement are finally mocked by triumphant bestiality" (Achebe 1989, 3). Of course, this *other world* is not genuine otherness, which is never so different as to be something like the missing link. This other world was the creation of an *actus reflexus* that had leaped over the barrier indeed. Caustically, Achebe writes in that regard: "For reasons which can certainly use close psychological inquiry, the West seems to suffer deep anxieties about the precariousness of its civilization and to have a need for constant reassurance by comparison with Africa" (17). Other literary critics have argued that the novel means well: *Heart of Darkness,* like *Uncle Tom's Cabin,* means to bring to light the indignities of human cruelty and human greed. Still, as with Stowe's work, Conrad's is mired in racism in a way that brings to light, I think, the racism Bonhoeffer sought to overcome.

I think too that *Heart of Darkness* gives another angle of vision on the central arguments of Bonhoeffer's early theology: (1) That the self-enclosed, and therefore all too subjective, vaunting of sameness results in the abuse of the Other — meaning both God and other people; and (2) That whether one sees, and really sees, the Other before reflecting on the meaning of that first sighting depends upon whether one has seen Christ.

Marlow, the protagonist of *Heart of Darkness,* sees the "heathen" African at the helm of a steamship "there below" him on the Congo River. To *look at* this African — remember the alienated *actus direc-*

tus — says Marlow, was about as "edifying" as watching a circus dog decked out in costume. Marlow thought this African would have been out in the bush with the thoroughly benighted others. But the civilization he could not master bewitched him and had made him better: "He was useful because he had been *instructed*" (emphasis added). Despite his heathen accoutrements — "an impromptu charm, made of rags, tied to his arm, and a piece of polished bone, as big as a watch, stuck flatways through his lower lip" — this African "was an improved specimen; he could fire up a vertical boiler." But he was only diligent because he assumed that a powerful spirit made the steamship go, and that should he forsake his work, the demon would anger and exact a terrible vengeance (Conrad 1970, 100-101).

We learn nothing about the scope of being from Marlow — the metaphysician — for we learn nothing about the *African*. We learn something about the self-enclosed I, and that there is, to quote Bonhoeffer, no "Christian I-Thou relation." For in seeing the useful African as *an improved specimen,* Marlow exemplifies a critical dimension of *The Communion of Saints:*

> Not every self-conscious I knows of the moral barrier of the Thou. It knows of an alien Thou — this may even be the necessary prerequisite for the moral experience of the Thou — but it does not know this as absolutely alien, making a claim, setting a barrier; that is, it does not experience it as real, but in the last resort it is irrelevant to its own I. (SC, 44-45)

It is only because Marlow sees the African as beneath him — as someone who makes no true claim on him — as someone superfluous to his own I — that he can turn the African into what is unreal: "He was there below me, and, upon my word, to look at him was as edifying as seeing a dog in a parody of breeches and a feather hat, walking on his hind legs" (Conrad 1970, 100).

Marlow saw an illusion. Marlow made of the African what the African was not — an entity *(a dog in a parody of breeches and a feather hat, walking on his hind legs)*. But insofar as there was a genuine African beneath the fabricated one, "it follows that we are concerned here with realities transcending 'the entity'" (AB, 13).

This is an ethical concern in part; and Conrad provides insight into the problem that gives rise to such ethics as he explains that the motive in Africa was "robbery with violence, aggravated murder on a great scale, and men going at it blind — as is very proper for those who would tackle a darkness." The darkness was their own; and the revelation of that fact is Marlow's realization that the men who wished to domesticate the Thou in the heart of the Congo were

> no colonists; their administration was merely a squeeze, and noth-
> ing more. . . . They were conquerors, and for that you want only
> brute force — nothing to boast of, when you have it, since your
> strength is just an accident arising from the weakness of others.
> They grabbed what they could get for the sake of what was to be
> got. . . . The conquest of the earth, which mostly means the taking
> it away from those who have a different complexion or slightly
> flatter noses than ourselves, is not a pretty thing when you look
> into it too much. (Conrad 1970, 69)

Well — the darkness was their own; and it was ugly.

The only thing that made such ugliness attractive was illusion: "What redeems it," this ugliness — wrote Conrad — "is the idea only. An idea at the back of it; not a sentimental pretense but an idea; and an unselfish belief in the *idea* — something you can set up, and bow down before, and offer a sacrifice to . . ." (Conrad 1970, 69, emphasis added). Truly, the idea of heathen Africa — and Bonhoeffer says as much in his short discussion of the "Negro" past — reveals more about a certain I than the diversity of the African Thou(s).

Bonhoeffer also noted that this caricature of Africanness was made all the more useful in the New World. Freed from sinful, primitive ways through baptism — here but a rite of acculturation

— the Christianized African would become more serviceable as a slave; for baptism *was found to have the advantage of keeping the slaves more easily under supervision than if they were left to continue their own pagan cults. Heart of Darkness* gives us the horrible poetry of it — as *cor curvum in se. Cor curvum in se* positively: For the Africans-beneath-the-Negro Bonhoeffer encountered were not "strings of dusty niggers with splay feet," but cultured Africans of West and Central Africa. One must see this in order to transcend the entity — the racist caricature of black being — and to appreciate the reality of those who were enslaved. One must see that

> Negroes . . . brought to bear numerous aspects of their varied African experience. The term "carryover" (which anthropologists have applied to objects as tangible as the banjo and to beliefs as vague as spiritualism) fits a range of techniques and insights which were probably retained in the eighteenth century and which will only be fully explored as we learn more about the parent cultures from which these slaves were taken. Unlike the local Indians [sic], for example, numerous Negroes possessed a familiarity . . . with the herding of stock and the cultivation of rice. Nor would indigo and cotton be strange plants to many Africans in later years, as they were to most European and American workers. (Wood 1975, 119)

No, the plundered Africans were not heathen. In the words of the late Basil Davidson, their ways of life were eminently well-suited to their contexts. Theirs was a different reality, demanding adherence to the ancestors' wisdom —

> the fruit of painstaking observation and analysis of soils and seasons and all the manifest diversities of nature, including human nature. In short, they had to be severely reasonable within their own cultures, the very reverse of the blind dictates of superstition that nineteenth-century Europeans supposed to reign supreme on the "dark continent." (Davidson 1992, 81)

Oyo, Kongo-Angola, Benin, Dahomey, Ashanti were kingdoms, city-states — not centers of darkness. Neither shadowy piths nor pits without "reverence and morality," these highly organized kingdoms of West and Central Africa were blessed with commerce and industry. Skilled in mining, diving, textile manufacture, animal husbandry, iron smelting, and agriculture, especially agriculture — the cultivation of rice, indigo, millet, and the like — the Africans more than held their own during the early centuries of the slave trade.

As modernity's slave trade got going, primarily from the fifteenth to the early seventeenth centuries, West and Central Africa were on par with Europe. Europe, primarily Iberia, could not dominate things. The Africans contained the Europeans to the coastal waters of the Atlantic in those early centuries, for the impressive maritime cultures along the primary rivers, the Niger and the Congo, prevented penetration of the interiors.

That Europeans, early on, traded successfully in slaves at all is owed to the fact that these powerhouse kingdoms had a long tradition of enslaving Africans conquered in war. "The willingness of Africa's commercial and political elite to supply slaves should be sought in their own internal dynamics and history. Institutional factors predisposed African societies to hold slaves, and the development of Africa's domestic economy encouraged large-scale trading and possession of slaves long before Europeans visited African shores" (Thornton 1992, 125). Which brings me to Dahomey.

Dahomey will furnish the prototype of the African-beneath-the-Negro for three reasons, none of which privilege Dahomey over other regions of Africa from which black Americans are descended. First, it figured intimately in the work of Melville Herskovit's *The Myth of the Negro Past,* which was largely responsible for pointing out that black Americans have an African history that they yield when they are looked at closely. (Herskovits also makes that point in his *The New World Negro.*) Second, the African theologian Barthélemy Adoukonou, whom I noted in the introduction, because I find that he brings out the import of Bonhoeffer's emphasis on Thouness, has himself explored African alterity in terms of the Fon of Dahomey. Third, Bonhoeffer's theology itself commends this approach — for the sake of freedom.

I want to take some time to discuss the second and the third reasons as they, especially, bear on the theological dimensions of my theme, the African-beneath-the-Negro, linked as it is to the memory of Dahomey.

Freedom for Bonhoeffer was first and foremost a gift; a theological event whose meaning was summarized in the last two lines of the section entitled "Action" of his "Stations on the Way to Freedom":

> God's command is enough and your faith in him to sustain you.
> Then at last freedom will welcome your spirit amid great rejoicing.

All one needs to live life, which is unpredictable, is faith — the wherewithal to obey God's command to follow Jesus no matter what. Finally, freedom — the long-sought-after place the Afro-slaves called Zion in their spiritual "Now Let Me Fly" — will welcome you.

> Way down yonder in the middle of the field,
> Angel working at the chariot wheel,
> Not so particular about working at the wheel,
> But I just want to see how the chariot feel
>
> Now let me fly
> Into Mount Zion, Lord, Lord.
>
> I got a mother in the Promised Land,
> Ain't going to stop till I shake her hand,
> Not so particular about working at the wheel,
> But I just want to get up in the Promised Land.

A slave is about to be free. But this God-given freedom demands ethics; knowing what to do:

Meet that Hypocrite on the street,
First thing he do is to show his teeth.
Next thing he do is tell a lie,
And the best thing to do is to pass him by.

One must bypass the duplicity that enslaves in God's name, but without assuming that freedom — meaning faith in a just God — and ethics are the same thing.

As Bonhoeffer put it in one of his early lectures:

> Ethics is a matter of blood and of history. But in that case how does the idea of a so-called *Christian ethic* stand? Are these two words, Christian and ethic, not perhaps completely disparate? Does not the idea "Christian" in this way become secularized, and the so-called Christian ethic become one alongside many, one of many, perhaps rather better or perhaps rather worse, but still in any event completely implicated in the relativity of history? In that case there is a Christian ethic as well as [an American] ethic, and neither of them is allowed to lay claim to superiority. It therefore seems to be extremely hazardous to speak of a Christian ethic and at the same time to maintain the absolute claim of such an ethic. (NRS, 36)

If, then, Christian is to ethics as the absolute is to the temporal — or the superior to the inferior — it is wise never to confuse them. They are related, however: What is *Christian* about ethics has to do with what has been given us: faith in Christ, and thus grace and hope, which are given in freedom. And — since ethics is a matter of blood and of history — freedom, which has not been given apart from the world's reality, concerns the bondage of African-Americans.

One wants to know (for Christ's sake!): What were black people before they came to America, before they sang sorrow songs in undeniable Protestant idiom? And why is the great put-down of their Old World being still an occasion for their bitter frustration and bewildered sorrow in the New World?

Bonhoeffer's legacy — particularly in regard to the break-through theology he was in quest of — pushes me to ask these questions. Should one not, for the sake of "apocatastatic" being, embrace the world, rejecting the racist metaphysics at the periphery?

Didn't my Lord deliver Daniel?
Deliver Daniel
Deliver Daniel?
Didn't my Lord deliver Daniel?
Then why not everyone?

Why *not* everyone? The question is eminently eschatological. Indeed, the spiritual calls to mind Bonhoeffer's sense of a true baptism, the meaning of which is found in *Act and Being,* and in terms of infant baptism.

His question is not whether babies can be Christians, but whether grace is free, unmerited, for everyone. If grace is so illimitable, then Thouness — infant or grownup, European or African — is never taken for granted, as if only adults, or only Europeans, were saved by Christ. Baptism, a true baptism, therefore pertains to who we are as persons, not merely what we are as objects; for (alien) subjectivity is the mystery of the Thou to the I, and the I to the Thou, and the I to the I — the basis of community, which is in God.

So why not examine Bonhoeffer's legacy in relation to Dahomey in order to understand better the enigmatic African-Americans he himself sought to embrace, as if they were in "heaven"? Why not do this for the sake of what Bonhoeffer called "the world-wide extent of our faith and hope," which cannot be imprisoned in any part of the world? Such myopia, that faith can be so imprisoned, assumes that *blood-and-soil* is equal to faith.

As Bonhoeffer has pointed out — for freedom's sake — "there are not and cannot be Christian norms and principles of a moral nature; the concepts of 'good' and 'evil' exist only in the performance of an action, i.e. at any specific present, and hence any attempt to lay down principles is like trying to draw a bird in flight" (NRS,

36). What has been given us — as Bonhoeffer pointed out years later in his *Ethics* — is not static, "something . . . fixed and possessed once and for all" (E, 39). What is more: "The will of God is not a system of rules . . . established from the outset; it is something new and different in each situation in life, and for this reason [one] must ever anew examine what the will of God may be" (38).

At the very least, that means, according to Bonhoeffer, that "when Jesus places [humankind] immediately under God, new and afresh at each moment, he restores to [us] the immense gift which [we] had lost, freedom" (NRS, 39). How this occurs is unpredictable; anything goes when one, in quest of the truth, has the strength (what has been given us) to defy convention. But truncate the truth through a narrow focus on *one* dimension of human experience, one set of ethical conundrums, and forfeit the freedom to seek the truth through the true encounter with the Thou. Truncate the truth and fail to see, the I is never the truth — for faith is "self-abolishing." It was in the light of this self-abolishing faith that Bonhoeffer was able to say: "Christian ethical action is action from freedom, action from the freedom of [one] who has nothing of himself and everything of . . . God, who ever and again lets . . . action be confirmed and endorsed by eternity" (39).

Eternity means, at least, God is no respecter of persons; that truth, while incarnate in the midst of us, is given *extra nos* (from outside of us). From the perspective of eternity, nothing — to make an allusion to Acts 11 — is unclean. And concomitantly, from eternity's perspective — to make an allusion to Romans 5:12 — nothing is clean; not Dahomey; not Germany; not America. God is no respecter of persons; for, as Bonhoeffer realized, God is *pro nobis,* "for the whole world — in America and Germany, in India and in Africa" (NRS, 73).

From eternity's perspective, the cross means "we all belong to one another," that we share the same origin and destiny. "Before the cross of Christ and his inconceivable suffering," wrote Bonhoeffer, "all our external differences disappear" (73). But not to the extent that they are inconsequential to the realization that we all belong

101

together. As I have stated in my Preface, alterity, otherness, is the precondition of the attainment of our common source and common lot.

The African theologian Barthélemy Adoukonou is akin to Bonhoeffer in believing that this freedom to belong together has been given to us through the cross — that because of the cross, theologies (so limited by "blood and soil") should not be intimidated by difference, the enigma of the Other.

Adoukonou's *actus reflexus* stems from his own revisiting of Dahomey, for he seeks to explore alterity, the dissonance of I and Thou, Same and Other — *du même et de l'autre* — through the scandalous juxtaposition of Christianity and Vodun (Dahomey's traditional religion). His point is that Vodun, construed in terms of old Dahomey *(la société traditionnelle dahoméenne)* is itself based on alterity, *la différence.* "One can say," he writes, "that one of the fruits of the ancestral experience of Vodun [meaning the gods] is that one becomes conscious of the necessity of respecting the divine mystery" (Adoukonou 1980, 283, my translation). Key to an understanding of such religion — which is but a stepping stone to faith for Adoukonou — is this realization: "Old Dahomey affirms and gives life to dissonance — God is not man, and Vodun is the *différance,* in the sense that Derrida gives that word" *(la société traditionnelle dahoméenne affirme et donne à vivre la* différence: *Dieu n'est pas l'homme, le Vodun est la* différ-ance, *dans un sens assez proche de celui que Derrida donne à ce terme)* (284).

According to Adoukonou, the Fon have appreciated this difference without understanding it eschatologically in Christ until their baptism. (As one old African put it, having been enslaved in America, "We know it a God, you unner'stand, but we don't know He got a Son.") And Adoukonou has sought to make that Fon appreciation — *we know it a God* — clear in terms of Chalcedon, the classic definition of Christ's person.

For Adoukonou — as for Bonhoeffer (and I have suggested as much in the introduction) — Chalcedon is that understanding of I and Thou, that understanding of alterity, surpassing all others.

To quote him, "The mediation of alterity that the church offers to the world through the ages remains that of Chalcedon — without separation or confusion" (Adoukonou 1984, 304, my translation). For both Adoukonou and Bonhoeffer, Chalcedon embraces scandalous difference as grace. To quote Bonhoeffer: "The mystery is left as mystery and must be understood as such. The approach is preserved for faith only. . . . One cannot form a concept of God and then draw boundaries within it" (CTC, 87-88). One who would pigeonhole God in that way also truncates the world and diminishes life.

In that regard, the child — so open to the world and to otherness — figures prominently in Bonhoeffer's *Act and Being*. The child, he argues, "is neighbor to the *eschata*." That is: "Willingness to be determined by the future is the eschatological possibility of the child." Despite her angst, "gripped by the onrush of things to come," the child is stayed on the present; while the jaded adult "lapses into the past, into himself, into death and guilt" (AB, 182).

For all his analysis of the traditional Fon, Adoukonou makes a similar point. (Adoukonou does not study the Fon for the sake of African traditional *religion!*) His goal is also the eschata *(trying to make heaven home)*. Adoukonou explains that the reigning symbolism of the Fon's passionate commitment to life is the child (more so than the ancestor); and it is only in relation to the Promised Land (Zion) that the child symbolizes life's triumph over death.

As it was for Bonhoeffer, then, so it is for Adoukonou: Reality means that the eschatological moment is given, now. Bonhoeffer put it this way: "In faith the future is the present; but inasmuch as faith suspends itself before the future . . . [humankind] 'is' in the future of Christ, i.e., never in actless being, never in beingless act" (AB, 182). Adoukonou puts it like this (and I paraphrase): The Fon have been called to decide for faith now, in the present, for since Christ, the eschatological moment is in the present . . . now (Adoukonou 1984, 307).

To be in Christ is to have an ultimate tomorrow, the eighth day, today — it is to be there:

> Why don't you sit down?
> Can't sit down!
> Sit down, I told you!
> I can't sit down.
> Go 'way don't bother me,
> I can't sit down
> 'Cause I just got to heaven
> And I can't sit down!

Whether one is from Germany or Dahomey, whether one is European, or African, heaven is home. . . .

This digression, this free association of Bonhoeffer and Adoukonou, makes the point that the African-beneath-the-Negro is integral to a reappraisal — a *reprendre* indeed — of Bonhoeffer in light of the problem of racism. In rejecting unilateral concepts of God and the drawing of boundaries regarding how to appreciate Bonhoeffer — and how not to appreciate him — I advance to freedom. For in Bonhoeffer's own words:

> Arbitrary deprivation of liberty, such as the seizure of defenseless and innocent people (for example when African negroes [sic] were hunted, captured and transported as slaves to America) and other forms of arbitrary imprisonment, constitutes a violation of the liberty which is given with the human body. When a man is forcibly and wrongfully separated from his home, his work and his family, and is prevented from exercising all his bodily rights and treated as though he were guilty of some crime, then he is being deprived of the honor which is associated with bodily liberty. (E, 185-86)

So we are brought back to Dahomey, to *the seizure of defenseless and innocent people*.

Dahomey, like any part of the continent from which the African-American comes, was no *jardin* of milk and honey. Especially for those outside of the leisure classes. As has been noted, Dahomey was a nation in which slavery was rife for the sake of the king, who enjoyed tremendous power and whose prerogative it was to demand human sacrifice. Slaves, derived from war and conquest, were more so than land the measure of the king's wealth and the means by which perks were procured for the leisure classes — "the King, the princes, the chiefs, the Priests, and the diviners. None of these were productive in the sense that farmers or iron-workers or cloth-workers [were] productive workers, but there was appropriated to them the social surplus derived from the labor of the great mass of Dahomeans, and more particularly . . . the masses of slaves" (Herskovits 1967, 97).

That lives were dispensable for the king's pleasure is another example of the tyrannical I. "Now he is lord of the world, but only of the world which his I interprets and fabricates for itself. . . . He sees his fellow as a thing and sees God as the one who satisfies his religious need, and now he seeks to set himself eternally in this world; he does not wish to die, he wishes to make himself right and to live forever" (NRS, 62).

Still, Dahomey, like several kingdoms of Lower Guinea, was highly organized and differentiated. Hunting guilds, farming guilds, blacksmithing guilds were all regulated through an impressive social polity. The fiscal polity was meticulously administrated. Each village head fastidiously watched over and took precise account of tributes to the king. Tribute, whether as livestock, produce, or bounty from the hunt, also took the form of tolls mandatory from province to province. Villages were composed of extended families and graced by a collective spirit demanding well-established protocol.

Whole communities had achieved longevity from well-considered mores that demanded respect of the neighbor and deferment to elders. The Fon language was highly sophisticated, well suited to communicate the nuances of the Fon's cosmos. Names had meaning, as did titles and terms of endearment for those holding esteemed positions. It was especially in Fon religion that the Dahomean cosmos was articulated with nuance and refinement. The rituals, the

105

people's *esprit du corps,* with its etiquette and mores; the artifacts that signify religiosity with rare sensitivity and exquisiteness (noted well by world-class museums); the fiber of the cosmos itself (the stuff out of which material culture was made) — all meant that life was to go on vital, potent.

Surely, it bears repeating that slavery, human sacrifice, and a diehard caste system revealed that life was hardly unfettered. But the whole of the Fon world should not be scrapped as heathen for that (no more than the whole of England should be totaled because of its trade in slaves)! Certainly, failure to consider Fon civilization as an antidote to *Heart of Darkness* (and other views emblematic of the myth of the Negro past) is to entertain questions with serious ramifications.

Is it really the case that the blacks Bonhoeffer encountered were better off as second-class citizens in America than if they had been left alone in Africa? Is it really the case that the Africanness beneath the spirituals Bonhoeffer loved was no more than a voodoo barbarism? Or do we, taking Bonhoeffer's lead, learn something about the Other when that Other is freed from the imperial Same, when one sees the integrity of the African past as the Thou?

I think we learn something about the Thou: To have lived linked to the ancestors, to remember in ritual the departed, to make sky and earth an extension of child, woman, and man was — explained Melville Herskovits — "the choice between oblivion and continued existence in the altruistic rôle of jealous guardian of the welfare and greatness of a person's descendants" (1967, 194).

The very fact that African theologians, such as Adoukonou, are exploring, as "faith-wishfulness" — I am using the word heuristically — this heartfelt drive toward "continued existence" is itself a sign that the African Thou expands the ramifications of Bonhoeffer's *Act and Being.*

To speak of the *actus directus* which may never be captured by reflexion (not my own act by myself, not to mention any second observer), to speak of infant baptism, of a self-abolishing faith, all this may appear to open prospects wherein not all roads are barred to the eschatology of an apocatastasis. Yet this very talk of apo-catastasis may not be much more than the wishful regret of the-ology, when it must speak of faith and unbelief, of election and rejection. (AB, 183)

Who knows who as well as what are heathen — meaning benighted and backward? That judgment is not ours to make — particularly when none of us sit where God sits in the matter *of election and rejection.* Until the eighth day, is it not better to extend to others the freedom we grant to ourselves within the limits of those mores conducive to liberty for all?

For the fact remains that the Negro of Bonhoeffer's day, in having been "de-heathenized," was dehumanized as well — and all in ser-vice to the Christian religion. How sad it is that the African Other in the New World has been vitiated in service to a society blessed and kept by the American church. How incestuous is that American context that has changed the Others' names, shorn them of dignity, and put them daily behind the curse of the eight ball. How pathetic it is — and how deadly! — that the African Other, transmogrified into the Negro of Bonhoeffer's day, has been shorn, neutralized, and frozen so that the Same might be the Same — "not enslaved, but free; not repulsive, but desirable; not helpless, but licensed and powerful; not history-less, but historical; not damned, but innocent; not a blind accident of evolution, but a progressive fulfillment of destiny" (Morrison 1992, 52). No catechism, Reformed or otherwise, can blot out the immorality that chained Africans' being in making them conform to a New World, "Christian" religion.

Americans, black and white, have an aversion to history in that regard, a susceptibility to an amnesia that resists drumming up the painful past in order to obtain insight into the painful present. For instance, how strange — even crazy — one appears who thinks of the Middle Passage as the reigning symbol of what the Negro is. Yet Bonhoeffer thought that "by sheer grace, God will not permit us to live even for a brief period in a dream world. [God] does not abandon us to those rapturous experiences and lofty moods that come over us like a dream. God is . . . the God of truth. Only that . . . which faces . . . disillusionment, with all its unhappy and ugly aspects, begins to be what it should be in God's sight, begins to grasp in faith the promise that is given to it" (LT, 27).

It is in that regard that it bears repeating that past events still loom as revelations of the horridness still with us. To quote Bonhoeffer again — for I have quoted these very same words in chapter two — *What is past, as "having" happened, is "background," unless the annunciation "coming to" us in the future should raise it to "presence"* (AB, 119). If Bonhoeffer is correct, Christ himself raises this background to presence. Yes: To the extent the sorrow songs are occasions to consider the emptiness of the Christian religion for Christ's sake, they call to mind the Middle Passage. The African novelist Yambo Ouologuem's *Le devoir de violence (Bound to Violence),* which is in part a critique of slave-holding and slave-trading Africa, makes my point.

A hundred million of the damned . . . were carried away. Bound in bundles of six, shorn of all human dignity, they were flung into the Christian incognito of ships' holds, where no light could reach them. And there was not a single trader of souls who dared, on pain of losing his own, to show his head at the hatches. A single hour in that pestilential hole, in that orgy of fever, starvation, vermin, beriberi, scurvy, suffocation, and misery, would have left no man unscathed. Thirty per cent died en route. And, since charity is a fine thing and hardly human, those amiable slavers were obliged when their cargo was unloaded to pay a fine for every dead slave; slaves who were as sick as a goat in labor were thrown to the sharks. Newborn babes incurred the same fate: they were thrown overboard as surplus. . . . Half naked and utterly bewildered, the niggertrash, young as the new moon, were crowded into open pens and auctioned off. There they lay beneath the eyes of the all-powerful (and just) God, a human tide, a black mass of putrid flesh, a spectacle of ebbing life and nameless suffering. (Ouologuem 1971, 12)

There — *in the Christian incognito of the ships' hold* — was no Christ; and in this specific sense: Neither the slave-trading Africans nor the slave-trading whites had their inward eye directed toward the bound and bewildered slave — the Other. How fitting it is, then, to consider the slaveships' stench as the symbol of what was in store for the *Africans*. One caught a whiff of their arrival when the vessel was miles offshore.

As I have argued, that bound and bewildered otherness accounts in fair measure for the plaintiveness of the sorrow songs — a plaintiveness so arresting because so alien in the New World. Until today, I hear a longing for home (where one can be oneself), in every strain, a longing that Zora Neal Hurston, the African-American anthropologist, caught in her interview with an elderly man, Cudjo Lewis. His real name was "Kossola-O-Lo-Loo-Lay" — seized when nineteen by the fierce Dahomean women-warriors of legend. Kossola landed in the United States as late as 1859. Hurston recounts the vividness of the man's sorrow in being plundered from home.

"I lonely for my folks. They don't know. Maybe they ask everybody go there where Kossola. I know they hunt for me." "After seventy-five years," wrote an astonished Hurston, "he still had that tragic sense of loss. That yearning for blood and cultural ties. That sense of mutilation. It gave me something to feel about" (Hurston 1984, 204).

What are the implications of subjecting human beings to such grief? What are the implications of ignoring the horror of it because of the illusion that Africans are but "niggertrash"? Surely the grief-stricken ones' suffering adds depth to Luther's dictum that Bonhoeffer liked so well — to paraphrase, the curses of the godless can be more pleasing to God's ears than the hallelujahs of the pious.

The Africans were thought to be heathen, Godless, and their signs and sounds and symbols akin to profanity; which adds rather than subtracts from their Christian import. For — remember this bit from *The Communion of Saints* — the kingdom of Christ pertains to those *elected in Christ*. But the kingdom of God pertains to *all the predestined*. Bonhoeffer's distinction stresses the limitations of the church, does not negate the claim that God is in Christ, and argues that no mortal, no matter how "Christian," knows exactly, if at all, who's who in heaven. What more so than that — the likelihood that the Africans were in God, *from eternity to eternity,* despite the racist view that were not — would serve as their call to Christianity? Which is all the more the case given Bonhoeffer's *Ethics,* particularly his understanding of what it means to say "the West" — which had solely to do with its formation in Christ, who hardly contradicts the scope of God's kingdom. The black church in America has made a great contribution in regard to this formation in Christ; and at its very beginning, at the dawning of the antebellum period, a certain "promising godlessness" — which Bonhoeffer related to the curses of those thought to be unGodly — laid, perhaps, the only true Western heritage the American church may claim.

W. E. B. Du Bois has made a compelling case for the view that the leader of the "primitive" black church was not a well-catechized divine, but a priest-diviner, whose power in "the African state" was enormous. Holding sway over "the province of religion and medicine," the priest-diviner, asserts Du Bois, emerged as the leader of the enslaved and "found his function as the interpreter of the supernatural, the comforter of the sorrowing, and as the one who expressed . . . the longing and disappointment and resentment of a stolen people" (Du Bois 1971, 255-56). Harold Courlander's novel *The African* brings this to light.

Occurring somewhere between the dusk of the eighteenth century and the dawn of the nineteenth, Courlander's tale is about a Fon boy, Hwesuhunu, who is sold into slavery under the tyrant King Adanzan. Landing in Savannah, Georgia, learning over time the ins and outs of slave culture, Hwesuhunu — his Negro name in the novel is *Wes* — seeks out Samba: precisely that figure Du Bois has written about. Guardian of an identity under siege, Samba comforts his cruelly uprooted sibling-slaves. He is Du Bois's preacher insofar as he conducts rituals that are life and health to a people *a long, long way from home.*

Hwesuhunu seeks Samba out because the memory of how the

Africans died wears Hwesuhunu out: "Doumé the ironworker, killed by the white folks. His people was Nago. Dokumi the hunter. His people was Nago. Koba was a Nago too. Dosu, he was a Fon like me. Osamba, named like you, Uncle, he was killed by the white people. Many, many dead, Uncle" (Courlander 1993, 101). Hwesuhunu wants them to be remembered properly: "Uncle, those people never had no proper service for them. . . . Someone has to fix it for them."

Samba agrees to perform the rite that lays the spirits to rest — the rite of healing that seeks valiantly to salvage what can be pieced together of an African's alterity:

> "Friends and cousins," Samba said, "this thing tonight is for the dead. Some of us been born here in Georgia, but some come from Africa. Wheresoever we been born, we got kinfolk in that old place and 'mongst the dead. Now you knows that the older a person get, the more respect you got to give him. Why is that? It's because an old man or woman is closer to the dead, that's why. Soon he will be 'mongst the dead. And the dead must be respected as much as the orishas and the vodouns [the gods]. If you don't do right by them, why they goin' to do right by you? You forget them, and they goin' to forget you too when you in need. That is why we brings a gourd of rice to the grave each year, so the kinfolk knows we don't forget." Samba was interrupted by fervent cries of "Amen." He went on: "This boy Wes Hunu. . . . He is only a boy, but he has the know that lots of folks already forget. The dead we remember tonight is many. Let us start with a prayer." He continued: "All you orisha, and Jesus too, we ask you to look way down here. See all these black folk on this plantation and listen to what they got to say. We know all people has to die, and us live ones ask for blessing." (Courlander 1993, 107)

The *Amens — and Jesus too —* suggest "Christians" were gathered there. They recognized that priest-diviner Samba was sharing with them what the catechism would take away — their Thouness, their

111

part to play in dissonance — the connection to home. *Again:* Scholars I regard highly (Hurston, Du Bois, Herskovits, John Lovell, Marshall Stearns, Miles Mark Fisher, Sterling Stuckey, to name but a few) make the point that the spirituals, which Bonhoeffer was taken by, emerged, precisely, from that connection to home. Du Bois put it this way in his classic essay "Of the Faith of the Fathers": "Sprung from the African forest, where its counterpart can still be heard, it [the spirituals, "music of Negro religion"] was adapted, changed, and intensified by the tragic soul-life of the slave, until, under the stress of law and whip, it became the one true expression of a people's sorrow, despair, and hope" (Du Bois 1969, 212).

Slaves with an impressive mastery of Protestant doctrine were certainly not rare. But the point of the sorrow songs is not doctrinal, for doctrine is susceptible to what one wants it to mean. "If," wrote Bonhoeffer in *Act and Being,* God is "within a doctrine," God may be domesticated — "understood and allocated [a] place in human 'existence'" — much in the same way one enslaves other persons in accordance with a worldview (AB, 108f.). The point of the sorrow songs is that a beleaguered folk thirsted for righteousness. In the immediacy of that thirsting, Jesus — if Bonhoeffer has any credibility — could have well come to them.

Remember Bonhoeffer's point regarding one's genuine encounter with Jesus? *Nothing could be more mistaken than to deny . . . that there is an* actus directus *taking place in time. For such a dismissal reflexion has no justification* (AB, 141).

> Who found me when I was lost?
> Who helped me to bear my heavy cross?
> Who fixed me up, turned me around,
> Left my feet on solid ground?
> I know it was Jesus!
> I know it was the Lord!

Analogous to that *actus directus* taking place in time — *I know it was Jesus!* — is the fact that the spirituals were a revelation of injustice, the lack of freedom, not of whatever catechism the slaves happened to encounter. That is, the claim of the Other — *I am a Thou, not a slave* — is a far greater reality than a New World catechism: The reality of injustice — the thirst for freedom — is closer to the reality of faith than it is to doctrine.

If, moreover, Bonhoeffer were correct that "Whether faith *is* faith can be neither ascertained nor even believed, but the faith which believes *is faith,*" then the spirituals would call us to reconsider his sense of the middle (AB, 148). The middle is where Christ is. And that middle is, in a sense, where the periphery is: God, Bonhoeffer explained, has allowed reality to be "pushed out of the world on to the cross" (LPP, 360).

In the slave quarters, a sense of being pushed out of the world was expressed in a spiritual that a Finkenwaldian, Heinz Neumann, remembers Bonhoeffer sharing (Day 1975, 515):

> Nobody knows the trouble I see,
> Nobody knows but Jesus.
> Nobody knows the trouble I see,
> Glory Hallelujah.

Trouble and glory, extreme alienation (*nobody* knows the trouble *I* see), and Jesus *(Glory hallelujah)* make the point that one is centered in Christ when he or she is "on the outer edge of the cosmos . . . confronted with the kingdom of God" (Barth 1967, 191). But this "outer edge" is the middle. The center of truth, the cross, only appears to be pushed *out* of the world.

To quote Bonhoeffer: "The stem of the Cross [has become] the staff of life, and in the midst of the world life is set up anew upon the cursed ground. In the middle of the world the spring of life wells up on the wood of the cross and those who thirst for life are called to this water, and those who have eaten of this wood of life shall never hunger and thirst again" (CF, 93-94). They may thirst after being flayed, go hungry for lack of bread, but never experience want because they turn from the suffering God. American slavery, with its attempt to purge life of Africanness in order to be content with a vitiated version of the Same, was run by highfalutin gentry tragically hostile to the middle where the kingdom comes.

Suffering is the center. Humankind knows its God and itself in suffering, in Christ — in the memory of the *actus directus*. The power of this is once more reflected in a sorrow song.

> They led Him to Pilate's bar,
> Not a word, not a word, not a word, not a word
>
> They cried, "crucify Him,"
> Not a word, not a word, not a word, not a word
>
> But He never said a mumbling word,
> Not a word, not a word, not a word, not a word,
> Wasn't that a pity and a shame?

The question does not refer to Jesus' humiliation but to those who, in ignorance as to the meaning of their actions, abuse him: They do not know what they do because their direct act is to themselves and not to the Other — not to God and to neighbor. But God is there in the serenity of unmerited suffering — a solemnity known when one is in the middle of injustice.

II
Bonhoeffer, Powell, an Ex-Colored Man, and Harlem

The African-Americans Bonhoeffer encountered at Abyssinian Baptist Church continued to sing their sorrow songs, for they were suffering. Having migrated from the Southland seeking the Promised Land, fleeing the violence against them and the cul-de-sac of peasant servility (or having been in New York over the course of several generations), they found themselves in Harlem not even a century removed from slavery's drudgery.

The upshot was the same: economic subservience and a well-enforced social caste that was Jim Crow all over again; many felt as trapped in Harlem as they had in Dixie. The Great Depression of the 1930s made their lives all the more difficult. In Abyssinian, founded in 1808 by Ethiopian merchants — they "had attempted to worship in a local white Baptist church and were insulted by being herded to the back upstairs" — the problem was never on the back burner (Hamilton 1992, 73).

After all, the powerhouse pastor was Adam Clayton Powell Sr., whose son, Adam Clayton Powell Jr., would become the celebrated master politician and congressman. Under the junior Powell, "the Abyssinian pulpit became the most politically outspoken in America" (Anderson 1983, 23). The elder Powell was born in Virginia in 1865. So Euro-looking that he could have passed for white, Powell could have well fit the bill for James Weldon Johnson's *The Autobiography of an Ex-Colored Man*.

Perhaps Bonhoeffer's interest in that novel had to do with the Powells he surely encountered. Perhaps James Weldon Johnson was the writer Bonhoeffer wrote about to his grandmother:

> I have again just finished a quite outstanding novel by a quite young Negro. In contrast to the rest of American writing, which is either cynical or sentimental, I find here a very productive strength and warmth, which continually arouses in one a desire to meet the man himself. (Bethge 1985, 109)

At any rate, Bonhoeffer wrote an essay on *Ex-Colored Man* for Reinhold Niebuhr, the world-class ethicist and renowned professor at Union Theological Seminary. Bonhoeffer concluded his essay as follows: "According to the whole mood in present Negro literature . . . it seems to me, that the race question is arriving at a turning-point" (109). (What an endorsement it is for Johnson's work that Bonhoeffer's quote *the race question is arriving at a turning-point* — which I quoted in chapter one — is owed to *Ex-Colored Man*.)

After the Ex-Colored Man (we do not learn his name) witnesses a lynching — "a scorched post, a smoldering fire, blackened bones, charred fragments sifting down through coils of chain; and the smell of burnt flesh" — he retires from public life into the privatistic, privileged world of a certain American religion. He explains his actions as follows: "A great wave of humiliation and shame swept over me. Shame that I belonged to a race that could be so dealt with; and shame for my country, that it, the great example of democracy to the world, should be . . . the only state on earth, where a human being would be burned alive" (Johnson 1990, 136-37).

So he forfeits his identity — a forfeiture symbolized by the love of his life, a woman "with lustrous yellow hair and eyes so blue as to appear almost black. She was as white as a lily, and she was dressed in white. Indeed, she seemed to me to be the most dazzlingly white thing I had ever seen" (144). And when he, under pain of much guilt, felt duty-bound to confess his "sin" to his beloved, his choice of words conveys the reality of an American contempt for blackness: "Then I told her . . . the truth. . . . Under the strange light in her eyes I felt that I was growing black and thick-featured and crimp-haired." His beloved, having at that point rejected his gift of love, made him feel for the first time in his life such "absolute regret at being colored, that [he] cursed the drops of African blood in [his] veins and wished he were really white" (149).

Adam Clayton Powell Sr. refused to pass, however. He had what Ralph Ellison defines as discipline, through which blacks

> recognize themselves as themselves despite what others might believe them to be. Thus, although the sociologists tell us that thousands of light-skinned Negroes become white each year, most Negroes can spot a paper-thin "white Negro" every time simply because those who masquerade missed what others were forced to pick up along the way: discipline — a discipline which . . . [most whites] would not undergo even if guaranteed that combined with their own heritage it would make of them the freest of spirits, the wisest of men and the most sublime of heroes. (Ellison 1972, 124-25)

Powell did not abandon the "earnestness and faith" that ennobled persons of indelible African descent in the New World. He never had occasion to say, "I have chosen the lesser part . . . sold my birthright for a mess of pottage" (Johnson 1990, 154). The issue for Adam Clayton Powell Sr. was never privilege, but freedom.

Because of Powell, Bonhoeffer taught Sunday school and worked in the various clubs of a church that was at the forefront of the struggle for freedom. For Abyssinian was a paragon of the black church that, to quote Powell, "from its beginning until now, has valiantly fought for freedom, justice and every principle of Christianity" (Powell 1938, 251). Some thirteen years before Bonhoeffer arrived on the Harlem scene, for instance, Powell admonished African-Americans not to rush headlong into World War I. Why, he argued, would a people take up arms for a nation that denied them "Constitutional rights as American citizens." He cited his people as being ten million, a multitude needed by the government. But this ten million needed to have "some assurance . . . of better treatment at home." "Why," asked Powell, "should not the colored Americans make a bloodless demand at this time for the rights [they] have been making futile efforts to secure [from a] government that has persistently stood by with folded arms while [they] were oppressed and murdered" (Anderson, 105)? Bonhoeffer was surely in the right place to understand that the Negro problem was *the* problem in America.

And there was more. The elder Powell embodied the rigorous revival-style preaching Bonhoeffer found impressive (NRS, 109). Powell Sr. learned this spirit-filled approach to the holy as a child, from the newly emancipated slaves. (Remember, Powell was born in 1865.) Exhibiting values and behavior learned from their ancestors, these ex-slaves kept their link to Africa alive. The clapping hands, polyrhythmic but sustained by a metronome sense; the ring-shout, the counterclockwise direction the slaves moved in when they, feeling the holy come on them, danced out a spiritual; the shrieks and moans, the convulsions that occurred when one was leveled by the holy — all were African at bottom.

In all probability, Powell's conversion experience is owed to that African continuum. He tell us in his *Against the Tide* that he, as a young man, made his way into a "Baptist church in time to see . . . the pastor . . . rise to take his text and fall to the floor under strong religious emotions. He did not utter a word, but it was the most effective sermon I have ever heard." The experience, wrote Powell, "sent an arrow of conviction to my wicked heart" (Powell 1938, 15). Whether the pastor was a member of the former slave community, I do not know. Nonetheless, Powell wrote that he "had often heard the ex-slaves pray that the day would come when the hillsides would be covered with mourners and the church doors would be crowded with young converts" (16). He felt he owed his own conversion to their prayers — the implication being that the ex-slaves had influenced the religious fervor that engulfed Powell himself.

Powell "believed in and encouraged 'shouting' services, where the parishioners would 'get happy' and express their emotion in open, often *frenzied* ways. Such displays of religious fervor were frowned on by some of the more sedate Negro churches, but not Abyssinian, where, in fact, at times, the effectiveness of the minister was as often measured in terms of the amount of noise and jubilation the preacher's sermons could arouse as in the numbers of converts and members attracted" (Hamilton 1992, 75; emphasis added). While likely to utter certain generalizations about the Negro — "All close students of religion and psychology agree that the Negro is enriching the church by his meekness, his simple, childlike faith and above all his generous emotional nature" — Powell embraced the African otherness at the heart of the Sanctified Church (Powell 1938, 270).

"When you see colored people leaping and jumping, running and shouting in the midst of some great religious service," wrote Powell, "the thing which moves them is not to be either crushed or criticized." While he thought this thing, which "makes them go wild and knock people down who happen to be in their way," needed tempering by way of a potent dose of American acculturation — "wait until they are properly refined" — he thought this thing was at the root of what would enrich the church (Powell 1938, 279-80). Connected intimately to the spirituals — *sprung from the African forest* — this thing lends credibility to the fact that Bonhoeffer encountered more than Negroes. Beneath them — these poor pilgrims of sorrow — was an African Other, the Thou. Powell, moreover, brings to mind Bonhoeffer's sense of the pertinence of the African past. "When I think," wrote Powell, "that the Negro was brought out of a jungle religion in Africa, into a worse jungle, American Christianity; when I recall that the Negro was not only brought here by racketeers, but that he existed for two hundred and forty years in the most damnable racket known in the United States, and that he has lived for the past sixty-five years in the racket of peonage, chain gang labor and industrial exploitation, it is a miracle that he has made any appreciable progress toward genuine religion" (Powell 1938, 255).

Bonhoeffer did not confine himself to Abyssinian alone. He was fascinated by *Harlem:*

> He spent nearly every Sunday and many evenings there. He took part in guided visits to the area, including a "trip to centres of Negro life and culture in Harlem," beginning with a flight over the district in which Negroes lived at a density of 170,000 to the square mile. (Bethge 1985, 109)

The Africanness hovering *ghostlike* at Abyssinian was all-pervasive in Harlem itself. For Harlem still had the whiff of Marcus Garvey about it. Garvey sought to return African-Americans bodily, but moreover ideologically and spiritually, to Africa. *Let Africa be our guiding star — our star of destiny!* exhorted the Jamaican-born Garvey. Garvey's significance was not lost on Abyssinian's senior pastor. He thought Garvey's coming to Harlem in 1914 was an event more significant than World War I, more significant than the great migration and than the struggles of Southern blacks to make it in the urban North. Envisioning a black republic, with black elected officials, a black defense, a black congress, a black God and a black theology, Garvey, argued Adam Clayton Powell Sr., was life itself to Harlem. "The cotton picker of Alabama, bending over his basket, and the poor ignorant Negro of the Mississippi Delta, crushed beneath a load of prejudice," wrote Powell, "lifted their heads and said, 'Let's go to Harlem to see this Black Moses.'" Because of Marcus Mosiah Garvey, thought Powell, Harlem was undeniably the black person's Mecca: "During the reign of Garvey there were two places in America — the Federation of forty-eight states and Harlem, and two million Negroes thought that Harlem was both of them" (Powell 1938, 70-71).

Surely all that has significance in light of Bonhoeffer's emphasis on freedom. Freedom, he would write later, is "a relationship and nothing else. In truth, freedom is a relationship between two persons. Being free means 'being free for the other,' because the other has bound me to him. Only in relationship with the other am I free" (CF, 37). One cannot be free in encountering the Negro depicted in Johnson's *Ex-Colored Man,* the protagonist of which remarks: "It is remarkable . . . what an adaptable creature the Negro is. I have seen the black West Indian gentleman in London, and he is in speech and manners a perfect Englishman. I have seen natives of Haiti and Martinique in Paris, and they are more Frenchy than a Frenchman. I have no doubt that the Negro would make a good Chinaman, with the exception of the pigtail" (Johnson 1990, 112).

That Negro was but a chameleon. No freedom there. But an *African*-American is the Other — the Thou without whom there is no community. Make no mistake, Bonhoeffer's impatience with students at Union Theological Seminary, who laughed out loud at Luther's *Bondage of the Will,* had much to do with Harlem's otherness. For in laughing at Luther, in being so unlike the shouting blacks in that regard, they had "evidently completely forgotten what Christian theology by its very nature stands for" (NRS, 87). But what might Luther have to offer in this regard?

III
The Bondage of the Will and
the Problem of Black Otherness

On the surface, *The Bondage of the Will* — *De servo arbitro* — is irrelevant to the problem of racism. Written in the sixteenth century, *De servo* took the Renaissance humanist Erasmus to task for his *De libero arbitro diatribe sive collatio (A Diatribe or Discourse Concerning Free Choice)*. Erasmus thought persons had a fair measure of free will. Lest they be puppets, and God an unfair manipulator, persons were to be blamed or commended for their vices or their virtues. Should they be virtuous, they merited God's blessing; but the onus for vice fell on the shoulders of the wrong-doer alone. "'Thou shalt'" do right "implies the indicative 'Thou canst'" do right, "and to deny the latter is to stultify the former" (intro. to Luther 1972, 9).

Erasmus did not question God's grace. He thought none could be saved without it; but grace that nullifies human freedom deprives salvation, as well as damnation, of its meaning. Luther thought Erasmus had failed to see that none is deserving, that none can do good and merit salvation. All merit damnation in Luther's book; the marvel is that God would save any.

Luther's view — that God's grace is so *Other* as to be totally alien to what human beings think is ethical — is downright funny in a racist world. Which white supremacist would not smirk at the claim that he has no free will, that God has determined whether he is truly good — and that he does evil when he thinks he is doing good? Which white supremacist would not find this claim amusing as well: Whether one hails from Dahomey or Great Britain has little to do with whether he is good.

The claim that we are valuable in accordance with pigment and background is, if we take Luther to heart, rubbish. That claim is, indeed, in Luther's words, "refuse or ordure being carried in gold and silver vases"; and that it is so makes certain people twitter a bit, or laugh derisively — perhaps to quell the uneasiness the truth musters in them (Luther 1972, 16)? An obvious problem here is that

121

Luther himself did not overcome a certain racism: William Shirer's *The Rise and Fall of the Third Reich* makes a compelling case for the view that Luther was a hero to Nazi Christians. Luther "wanted Germany rid of the Jews," writes Shirer, "and when they were sent away he advised that they be deprived of 'All their cash and jewels and silver and gold' and, furthermore, 'that their synagogues or schools be set on fire, that their houses be broken up and destroyed . . . and they be put under a roof or stable, like the Gypsies'" (Shirer 1992, 326-27).

Still, *Bonhoeffer* realized the implications of Luther's position — "the righteousness of God is revealed and avails for all and upon all who believe in Christ, and . . . there is no distinction [Rom. 3:21f.]." That is clear from Bonhoeffer's relationship to African-Americans (*and* Jews!). Remember too the significance of the *actus directus* in that regard — the reference to "the abject form in which the word of God comes" (Luther). For if one is stayed on Jesus, one realizes, racism is idolatry — that the racist holds to the merits of free will because he is a slave to himself, his sameness.

One has no choice in embracing the Other: one is bound either to Christ or to sin. The more one tries to abandon this either-or situation, the worse racism gets. Christians have no choice but to embrace it — lest someone, anyone, imply God is a respecter of persons. But, as Luther put it, his racism notwithstanding, "there is no *prosopolempsia* and God is no respecter of persons" (LW, 56). Those who overcome *Heart of Darkness,* who can embrace Dahomey as integral to the concept of civilization — meaning the concept of viable humanity — realize this. If God gives grace to the whole human race, what would any person lack who has God's grace? What do the black folk lack if God, from all eternity, has been no respecter of persons?

If all that is true, unwarranted hostility to Negroes, with Africa beneath them, has everything to do with a hostility to Christ. One may infer this — that hostility to blacks is hostility to Christ — from part of a letter that Bonhoeffer wrote Helmut Rössler, which is dated 11 December 1930.

122

I have seldom found it so hard to accept Christmas in the right way . . . my hope to find Heb. 12.1 fulfilled here has been bitterly disappointed. Besides, they find German theology so utterly local, they simply don't understand it here; they laugh at Luther. . . . (NRS, 67)

Quite an inference perhaps. One wishes that Bonhoeffer had said *they laugh at Luther, and that they do has nearly everything to do with their racism toward Negroes and, therefore, their hostility to Christ.*

I think, though, that Bonhoeffer says as *much* — at least if one reads his "The Negro Church," a section of his "Protestantism without Reformation," which reflects Bonhoeffer's life in Harlem. The segment of that section that I find most pertinent is "If it has come about that today the 'black Christ' has to be led into the field against the 'white Christ' by a young Negro poet [Countee Cullen undoubtedly], then a deep cleft in the church . . . is indicated" (NRS 108). Bonhoeffer clearly thought the whites had the primary responsibility to reconcile the racially divided church. And so what Bonhoeffer wrote bears repeating: *The solution to the Negro problem is one of the decisive future tasks of the white churches.* Why would the white churches bear primary responsibility in this unless it were so that they, above all, needed to see that their racism was, indeed, a hostility to Christ — the One standing on the boundary of the white I and the black Thou?

The fact, then, that Bonhoeffer says nothing about Harlem in his letter to Rössler hardly diminishes the fact that Bonhoeffer's *I have seldom found it so hard to accept Christmas in the right way* is related to the race problem. For it seems fair to say that he found the white Christ to be the icon of an American theology — a Christianity that is "essentially religion and ethics." What is clear is that Bonhoeffer was quite down at Christmas in 1930, which had much to do with his disillusionment with the white Christ. He felt alienated from the white Christians, not the black ones. For if he found Hebrews 12:1 — *Therefore, since we are surrounded by so great a cloud of witnesses, let us lay aside every weight, and sin which clings so closely, and let us run with perseverance the race that is set before us* — if he found that Scripture fulfilled anywhere, he found it fulfilled at Abyssinian. He was not so alone among the African-Americans.

With their intentions directed toward Jesus, they — Bonhoeffer and the Abyssinian saints — were *trying to make heaven home.* Not that they, *tossed and driven,* sought refuge in the religious by-and-by. Their by-and-by was a this-worldly by-and-by that in faith and hope would take the apostate world's best shot squarely on the chin.

CHAPTER 4

"I'm Going to Lay Down This Heavy Load":
Bonhoeffer's Costly Grace

O' by and by, by and by
I'm going to lay down this heavy load

I know my robe going to fit me well . . .
I tried it on at the gates of hell

By and by, by and by
I'm going to lay down this heavy load . . .

The sorrowful ones who awaited Bonhoeffer when he returned to
Germany in 1939 were the Jews grieved by a nazism on the move
and gathering steam. He had no choice but to respond to such
sorrow. Having been moved by the New World's African otherness,
having gained insight into the grief it caused, Bonhoeffer could not
well have turned a deaf ear to Jewish otherness, as if he could have
chosen, freely, to go the route of those who made the Jewish question
an *adiaphoron,* something optional for the faithful.

He realized that obedience to Christ and contempt for those like

125

him could not coexist. One could not be a Christian, with all that implies regarding Israel, and push Jews out of the church. For his refusal to live racist-ly — a mark of his election? — Bonhoeffer carried, in the words of the spiritual, a *heavy load*. His faith alone equipped him to carry it as a penultimate burden only — *by and by,* he would put it aside, for Christ's sake.

Bonhoeffer's final writings — *Christ the Center;* "The Leader and the Individual in the Younger Generation"; "The Church and the Jewish Question"; *Life Together; The Cost of Discipleship;* and *Ethics* — should, I think, be reread as his shouldering of this heavy load. I discuss them here as such — as records of the depth of Bonhoeffer's commitment to freedom, as testimony of the length he was willing to go to stand up to white supremacists, for Christ's sake.

I
Christ the Center; "The Leader and the Individual in the Younger Generation"; "The Church and the Jewish Question"; *Life Together*

For *Christ's sake* means that the after-Harlem theology through which Bonhoeffer made sense of his faith was christology, which involved a basic and incontrovertible question — "*Who* are you?" — found in *Christ the Center,* a book put together from Bonhoeffer's lectures on christology at the University of Berlin in 1933. When the question is asked religiously it amounts to "'How are you possible?,' that is the godless question, the serpent's question" (CTC, 30). For *How?* projects the I's shortcomings onto God's perfect Thou — questions the mysterious reality of God's incarnate love. What is more, "How?" says to people different from oneself, You are not really possible, have no place in redeemed creation.

When, however, the question *Who?* is posed in faith — "Who are you? Are you God?" — the questioner is gifted with revelation: God-in-Christ, alone, says yes; and "He answers only to the question 'Who?'" (CTC, 30). Where faith is given, "the question must

126

already have been answered before it could be stated correctly." For, "The question 'Who?' can only be put legitimately when the person questioned has revealed himself and has eliminated" the religious "How?" (31). Human beings cannot themselves ask "Who?" Faith alone can.

What is more, "The question, 'who?,' expresses the strangeness and the otherness of the one encountered and at the same time it is shown to be the question concerning the very existence of the questioner. He is asking about the being which is strange to his being, about the boundaries of his own existence" (CTC, 30). As he has argued in *The Communion of Saints,* and as he demonstrated in Harlem, Bonhoeffer implies in *Christ the Center* that God and sociality go together: The extent to which one can be content with God's ultimate alterity is the extent to which one can be content to live with others different from oneself. For Christ assumes the form of the other's enigma, stands before her in that sense — in the middle of I and Thou — and commands that one ask who and not how. Who, then, means that "it is only from God that [one] knows who he is." God alone frees one from the prison of the Same. Without God, the Same "remains related to itself and only mirrors itself in itself" (31).

Those who missed the ontological weight — meaning here the salvific consequences — of Jesus' *Who do you say that I am?*–question were bound to want to remove this questioner. Truly, "the one who compelled the dangerous question must be killed and with him the question" (CTC, 33). One might say that nazism as well as the American contempt of African-Americans have been but the desire to push God out of the world. So, "Christ goes through the ages, questioned anew, misunderstood anew, and again and again put to death" (35).

Think about Auschwitz's gas chambers: The unsuspecting victim had no idea of what was hidden beyond "well-kept lawns with flower borders; the signs at the entrances merely said BATHS. The unsuspecting Jews thought they were simply being taken to the baths for the delousing . . . customary at all camps. And taken to the

127

accompaniment of sweet music" (Shirer 1992, 1262)! At Auschwitz, a *Vernichtungslager*-hospitality (a death camp–hospitality) meant, to quote Bonhoeffer — if a tad out of context — that "Christ is still betrayed by the kiss. Wishing to be done with him means always to fall down with the mockers and say, 'Greetings, Master!'" Yes, "There are only two ways possible of encountering Jesus: [we] must die or . . . must put Jesus to death" (CTC, 35).

"But," wrote Bonhoeffer, "what happens if this Counter-Word, which was killed," namely Jesus Christ, the one who invalidates the racist word, "rises alive and victorious as the final Word of God" (CTC, 33)? If this be true, then racism cannot triumph, does not have the *last* word; for "one cannot avoid encounter with the person of Jesus because he is alive" (34). And that he is, Bonhoeffer believed, has to do with salvation indeed.

"Christology is not soteriology," however. We do not ask, "Who are you?" if we focus on Jesus' work rather than his person. That would confuse *act* with *being* (notwithstanding that both are one in Christ by virtue of *who* he is). The focus on work vitiates "person" as the cornerstone of sociality inasmuch as it would bypass the sovereignty of the Thou, place works before grace, fail to see the Being in whom all are without respect to human type. No, wrote Bonhoeffer, appealing to Luther's authority, "the person interprets the work" (CTC, 37). The implications of that for the problem of racism are disturbing.

Should one ask another, *How are you possible?* calling into question his so-called race, one, analogously, confuses works with person. For what one is ("race") — to the extent that it infers what one does, or can do (works) — is not necessarily who one is (person): A Nazi may hold that his Aryan-ness is his virtue — the good works he *thinks* he does, the good work he thinks he is. Forcing others into a permanent lower caste for no good reason but the color of their skin; finally purging that caste from the face of the earth — that is his virtue.

His intention to commit genocide notwithstanding, the racist may fancy himself a Christian. He goes to church regularly, tithes religiously, neither smokes nor drinks, is faithful to his family, and so on. Misconstruing four of the commandments — *You shall have no other gods; You shall not take the Lord's name in vain; You shall not kill; You shall not bear false witness against your neighbor* — the racist does "good" works. Placing works before person — meaning who he really is as he crushes the person-who-is-the-Other — the racist is the very opposite of the virtuous man he thinks he is.

The commandments to which he is blind say it all: The failure to honor *God;* the taking of God's name in vain in the making of graven images (the swastika); the desire to kill those who threaten the purity of the master race; and the bearing of false witness against them in the assumption that they are not genuine members of the human race — all indicate the absence of precious grace: Christ himself is discovered on the boundary of the other person, or not at all. Where Christ is present, one has to *do* nothing but keep the faith — a gift, not a work — the gift of God's self, the gift of the Other, an eminently personal endowment.

The deadly syndrome that confuses works with person has this ramification as well: In rejecting the one who is too black or too Jewish, et cetera — in asking, "How are you possible?" — one renders invisible whatever genuine virtue the rejected one has. Who he is, the kind of person he is, is erased in preservation of the Same. Without its pariahs, this vocation has no content: the despised ones define what is misconstrued as good works. They, the pariahs, furnish the Thou-shall-not that exercises bigoted morality. Work is so confused with person here that human beings — analogous to God in their nonobjectivity — are thought to be as unworthy as the thief, or the liar, and so forth. One might say: Black skin is to unworthiness as the lack of merit is to suffering. The innocent blood of many fine persons has been shed as a result.

Vulgarly, *Führer* Hitler summed up this ugly attitude in his *Mein Kampf:* "Was there any form of filth or profligacy, particularly in cultural life, without at least one Jew involved in it? If you cut cautiously into such an abscess, you found, like a maggot in a rotting body, often dazzled by the sudden light — a kike" (Hitler 1971, 57)!

Hitler's presumption was provoked by a person whose otherness was arresting (as in *actus directus*):

> Once, as I was strolling through the Inner City, I suddenly encountered an apparition in a black caftan and black hair locks. Is this a Jew? was my first thought. . . . I observed the man furtively and cautiously, but the longer I stared at this foreign face, scrutinizing feature for feature, the more my question assumed a new form: Is this a German? (56)

The Jew awakened Hitler to the depth of his anti-Semitism, his sameness, without which he himself would have had no identity. The Jewish man's person — his individuality, his *alien I* — was shackled by the illusion of his outward (ethnic) appearance.

"Later," Hitler wrote, "I often grew sick to my stomach from the smell of these caftan-wearers. Added to this, there was their unclean dress and their generally unheroic appearance" (Hitler 1971, 57). Which is to say: "How are you possible?" and, that nothing the Jews did was worth much:

> The Jew possesses no culture-creating force of any sort, since the idealism, without which there is no true higher development of man, is not present in him and was never present. . . . Not through him does any progress of mankind occur, but in spite of him. (303)

So fervently did Hitler covet the Aryan ideal that he believed that his anti-Semitism was *"the work of the Lord"* (65). How could Christ be a Jew?

Hitler had been influenced, in fact, by Houston Stewart Chamberlain, an Englishman and Aryan-lover, who wrote, "'Whoever claimed that Jesus was a Jew was either being stupid or telling a lie . . . Jesus was not a Jew.'" More than likely, argued Chamberlain, Jesus was an Aryan. Even if he were not an Aryan by blood, he *acted* like one "by reason of his moral and religious teaching," which was so unlike "'the materialism and abstract formalism' of the Jewish religion" (Shirer 1992, 155). Lost on Chamberlain and Hitler both was Bonhoeffer's claim that "there is no point in the life of Jesus of which one could say with unambiguous conviction that here we see the Son of God, proved to be such by one of his works. . . . The incognito of the Incarnation makes it doubly impossible to recognize the Person by his Works" (CTC, 38-39). That is, the God-man is veiled in the skin and bones — underneath a caftan-wearing Jew indeed — so foundational to the bigot's misappropriation of a person's worth. For who one is is more than flesh and blood; and that is why the one who questions aright understands Bonhoeffer's point: "So long as the christological question is the question of the human logos, it remains imprisoned in the ambiguity of the question, 'How?' But when it is given voice in the act of faith, there is a real possibility of posing the question, 'Who?'" (36).

A church that so misconstrued the relation of works and person, that had its soteriology confused with its christology; a church that asked the infernal *how*-question; a church that preached loyalty to the *Führer,* and the nationalistic imperative; a church that refused communion with Bonhoeffer's friend Franz Hilderbrandt and sent Bonhoeffer's *beau-frère,* Gerhard Leibholz, packing with his wife, Bonhoeffer's twin sister Sabine — that church could not question Christ, except to ask, "How?"

Who Christ is, however, is revealed in "the offensive form of preaching": Christ "is present as the risen and exalted one only in preaching; and that means only by way of a new humiliation" (CTC, 46). *Only by way of a new humiliation?* Are persons burdened with the Same the *imago Dei* (the image of God)?

The scandal for our time is that one may well argue yes — that resurrection is present, analogously, in the victims of racism. It became clear for Bonhoeffer, surely, that Christ was hidden in the Jews' misery — an ugly reality that heightened Bonhoeffer's realization that Christ was *pro me* (meaning *for me* and therefore for others). Christ is not tied to the particularities of his time; he is not, ontically speaking, a being-in-himself; he is, ontologically speaking, a being-for-others. Christians, who claim to follow him, must be for others as well.

For, "what is decisive about the *pro me* structure is that being and act of Christ are maintained together in it. *Actio Deo* and *praesentia Dei,* the *for you* existence and *being there* for you are joined together": *act,* because God *gives* humanity the gift of Christ; *being,* because God *is* the basis and the fullness of life that is given in Christ (CTC, 47). Nothing in Bonhoeffer's context illustrated the shrinking of being more than the Jews' misfortune. Murdered — with gas, fire, bullets, and starvation — by the millions before the Holocaust's end, the Jews were the victims of "Christians" who failed to see Christ-in-the-middle — the *pro me*–Jesus. Such Christians never asked the who-question. The upshot of their how-question was the shame of the "final solution."

It is to the credit of Bonhoeffer's God that Bonhoeffer confronted the Nazi menace *before* the Holocaust. In 1933, around the time that he lectured from the material on which *Christ the Center* depends, Bonhoeffer, in his "The Leader and the Individual in the Younger Generation," took the *Führer* to task. Bonhoeffer started this important lecture with the words: "Three brothers, of whom the eldest was born in 1900, the second in 1905 and the third in 1910, who are now 33, 28, and 23 respectively, today embody the difference between three different generations. Yet they all belong to what is usually called the 'younger generation'" (NRS, 186). Having lost his brother, Walter-the-first-generation, to World War I, Dietrich-the-second-generation knew well how deeply the First World War had scarred this "younger generation." The humiliating defeat that the Germans suffered in that war left too many of them thirsty for vindication, especially those of the third generation, who tended, suggested Bonhoeffer, to overcompensate for the fact that they had not the wizened wisdom of their older brothers, who bore the war's terror in their minds and bodies. The horror of this war — brought vividly to mind in the Paucks' biography of Paul Tillich, who suffered nervous breakdowns at the shell-shocked front — was borne by that generation as a badge of honor.

"For the older men," wrote Bonhoeffer, the negative ramifications of the war were "continually overcome in the actual course of life." They had paid their dues and knew the costliness of patriotic responsibility. The second generation had a lot to prove in that regard: It yearned for "the creation of a responsible situation in which this complex of problems might be experienced. Thus, precisely as a result of this encounter with their older brothers, the younger men were led to become creative; not so much to tolerate and maintain in responsible fashion what already existed, as to create, as a result of radical criticism, their own form of life."

The third generation had little to say about the weighty angst-provoking matters of national existence. "In conscious opposition to the volubility of the earlier generation in such matters, the ultimate questions of life are answered with silence." Not quite a silence of the grave, but a preoccupation with sports and the like — until the rise of the Führer (NRS, 188).

In him, the third-generation brother found his niche, and this was because he especially, but not exclusively, was vulnerable to a mass hysteria not unlike that which Bonhoeffer thought prevailed in the French Revolution. Times were such that "the problem of life losing its general questionableness, becoming quite definite, hardened into the question of political action." But, argued Bonhoeffer, this was no more than a "metaphysics of reality" (NRS, 188-89). It gave rise to a vitiated individualism and a vitiated collectivism.

As individuals (vitiated individuals) with no genuine sense of the Thou, especially the Jewish Thou, misled German I's prevailed in a mass enthusiasm (i.e., a vitiated collectivism). Bonhoeffer attributed that sorry state to "political-chilastic thought," a xenophobia — a sameness concentrated in the person of the Leader, the *Führer*. "The leader now becomes — and in the youth movement became in a very special way — the Leader of [one's] own, hitherto undiscovered, better self. In choosing a Leader the individual frees himself for himself. Being led, he now sees in the Leader his own, ideal, human ego" (NRS, 193). "The spirit of the people — so one imagines — summons the Leader from its metaphysical depths and raises him to the heights" (195).

So the rise of the *Führer* raised the Aryan-self to the status of a god, a god in whom the bluest eye prevailed, a god blind to Bonhoeffer's who-question implied in the pamphlet his good friend Franz Hilderbrandt wrote to oppose the rise of the German Christians:

> *The German Christians* say: The appearance of Jesus Christ in world history is in its ultimate significance a phenomenon of a Nordic character. (Jäger)

> The Bible says: The book of the genealogy of Jesus Christ, the son of David, the son of Abraham (Matt. 1.1). (quoted in NRS, 205)

Failing to see Christ in the Jews, the Nazi Christian could only ask: *How* is it possible for the Christ to be anything else but the apotheosis of an on-the-mend-and-thirsty-for-vindication Germany?

But such a false god would shatter, argued Bonhoeffer, and those who had enthroned that god would incur God's judgment, for "anyone who lays violent hands on man here is infringing eternal laws and taking upon himself superhuman authority that will eventually crush him" (NRS, 199). Those who would survive the crushing, thought Bonhoeffer, were saints who questioned Christ aright through word and sacrament. That *communio* was the rock on which Peter had built the church. Peter's *actus directus,* his inward eye, had recognized who Jesus — "the Christ, the Son of the living God" — is, the *pro me* savior.

In *Christ the Center,* Bonhoeffer asserts that "there is sacrament only when God, by his special Word, in the midst of his created world, addresses, names and hallows an element" (CTC, 53). This addressing, naming, and hallowing are in "the form of his humiliation or offence" (54). And — again — humiliation and offense translated for Bonhoeffer into the suffering of the Jews.

As Bonhoeffer would have it, the controversy over the Real Presence at the Colloquy of Marburg in 1529 brings to mind that real issue. At Marburg, Luther and Zwingli went at it over whether the ascended Christ was bodily present during the Eucharist. Luther said yes, for the ascended body of Christ had taken on the omnipresence of God's right hand. Zwingli said no, for to assume that Christ's body was at the right hand of God *and* under, around, and through the bread was to violate the integrity of Christ's human body.

Bonhoeffer finds Zwingli's position at the heart of the Reformed's *Extra-Calvinisticum,* a doctrine that has it that God-the-Son is incarnate but is nonetheless in essential relationship with Father and Spirit transhistorically, outside of the body in that sense (as in *finitum incapax infiniti*). To quote Bonhoeffer, the *Extra-Calvinisticum* assumes that "Christ, as the person of the Logos . . . existed outside the corporeal state" (CTC, 55). As such that doctrine exemplifies the *How?* approach to christology.

For Bonhoeffer, however, God is altogether here on earth — as God *and* as man (as in *finitum capax infiniti*). And he thought Luther was closer to the truth in this regard — to the *who*-approach to theology, to the fact that "the primary question in christology is not about the possibility of uniting deity and humanity, but rather about the concealment of the God-Man in his humiliation. God is revealed in the flesh but concealed in the stumbling block" (CTC, 54). While Bonhoeffer rejects Luther's doctrine of the *genus majestaticum* — that the "body of Jesus is not bound by space, but is present in all places at the same time" — he found that Luther grasped the point of God's reality (55). Luther's mistake, according to Bonhoeffer, was to abandon, after all, the who-question in favor of the how. Luther relinquished reality in favor of metaphysical speculation: Jesus Christ, God and man, Jesus Christ, the person, was given over to medieval talk of space, of mode, and of presence. Left undiscussed was the reality of "the presence of the God-Man, the person who is the one both exalted and humiliated" (57).

The question is, Who, precisely, is Jesus Christ for us today, given that he is the one both exalted and humiliated? One answer is to

135

insist that the victims of racism are not unlike the crucified Christ
— not because they are divine, but because their humiliation is
inseparable from the reality of the suffering-God-in-Christ. To
diminish the call of this suffering God is to deny reality: The Real
Presence is the enigma of the Thou, the Thou who suffers, who is
very, *very,* much on earth as in heaven.

Forget, then, the metaphysical constructs that obscure the relation
between the present Christ and the Other, who is known, however
indirectly, in the *spiritual* community. As Bonhoeffer put it in his
Life Together — a well-noted book from his Finkenwalde period:

> Within the spiritual community there is never, nor in any way,
> any "immediate" relationship of one to another, whereas human
> community expresses a profound, elemental, human desire for
> community, for immediate contact with other human souls, just
> as in the flesh there is the urge for physical merger with other
> flesh. Such desire of the human soul seeks a complete fusion of
> I and Thou, whether this occurs in the union of love or, what is
> after all the same thing, in the forcing of another person into one's
> sphere of power and influence. Here is where human ties, sug-
> gestions, and bonds are everything, and in the immediate com-
> munity of souls we have reflected the distorted image of every-
> thing that is originally and solely peculiar to community mediated
> through Christ. (LT, 33)

One who seeks such immediacy violates the Other in refusing to
grant him or her agapic space — the Other is invaded through the
coveting of the Same.

Racism is just such a coveting: In the refusal to accept Jews at the
communion table, *à la* the Aryan clause, apostate Christians disre-
garded their Lord. In asking, "How is it possible for Jews to have free
space at the Lord's table?" such Christians succumbed to a religious
whim; the desire to push God out of the world. This is why Bonhoeffer
wrote that to know who Christ is is to know where he is.

He stands for me, where I cannot stand; which "brings out clearly that I am separated from my 'I,' . . . by a boundary . . . I am unable to cross" (CTC, 60). This boundary — the *barrier!* — is grace: Bonhoeffer believed that Christ reminds us — until today — that we are fallen; and so he stands between us. Otherwise we descend deeper into the abyss, which is no myth but as real as the Holocaust, as real as the holocausts that assail us today. Failing to see that the meaning of history is "tied up with an event that takes place in the depth and hiddenness of a man who ended on the cross," racists lose touch with reality. "The meaning of history is found in the humiliated Christ" (62).

So Bonhoeffer knew what to do when idolatry gripped the nation and placed the swastika in the place of the cross. For Christ, the word, argued Bonhoeffer, "conveys unambiguous and clear meaning. Clarity and simplicity constitute his very nature. It is its own explanation. Clarity and simplicity are the reasons for its universal validity. Clarity and simplicity are of the very nature of the Word of God. The divine Logos is truth and meaning" (CTC, 49).

Simple, clear, meaningful truth. In 1933, that, for Bonhoeffer, was little more than the fact that a church, succumbing to an egregious racist metaphysics with no truth in it, would purify itself by expelling Jews, without whom there could be no body of Christ. Quoting Luther — "If the Apostles, who were Jews, had dealt with us Gentiles as we Gentile deal with Jews, there would have been no Christians among the Gentiles" — Bonhoeffer knew what to do. That is made clear in his "The Church and the Jewish Question."

While bound to a certain problematic view regarding Judaism, namely that Christianity superseded Judaism, he denounced the racist grounds on which Jews were excluded from the church. Bonhoeffer's friend Franz and his brother-in-law, Gerhard, were not *Jewish* Christians, but Christians — period. For, according to Bonhoeffer,

Judaism is never a racial concept but a religious one. What is meant is not the biologically questionable entity of the Jewish race, but the "people of Israel." Now the "people" of Israel is

137

constituted by the law of God; a man can become a Jew by taking the Law upon himself. But no one can become a Jew by race. (NRS, 223)

If, moreover, one is to understand the church's history and its theological implications for today, "it is not baptized Christians of Jewish race who are Jewish Christians." From the vantage point of an edifying ecclesiology, "the Jewish Christian is the man who lets membership of the people of God, of the church of Christ, be determined by the observance of a divine law. In contrast, the Gentile Christian knows no presupposition for membership of the people of God, the Church of Christ, but the call of God by his Word in Christ" (224). The pot called the kettle black.

II
The Cost of Discipleship

To know *who* Christ is is to follow him to where he calls from weakness. This is the message of Bonhoeffer's *The Cost of Discipleship*. Grace is "*costly* because it cost God the life of [the] Son . . . and what has cost God much cannot be cheap for us" (COD, 48). The impediment to this call, which Bonhoeffer called "the pure Word of Jesus," is that human beings erect so many *fraudulent* barriers to Christian discipleship — "human ballast — burdensome rules and regulations, false hopes and consolations — that it has become extremely difficult to make a genuine decision for Christ" (38). Religion gets in the way; metaphysics take over; human fellow-feeling abides — "Grace without price; grace without cost!"

The heavy load that grace put on Bonhoeffer's shoulders is inseparable from this memorable line in *The Cost of Discipleship: Only he who believes is obedient, and only he who is obedient believes.* That, in fact, was the import of Bonhoeffer's discussion of the lawyer figure in Luke's Gospel, who thought he could play games with Christ by attempting to undermine the call to discipleship — "Thou shalt love thy God with all thy heart, and with all thy soul, and with all thy strength, and with thy mind; and thy neighbor as thyself." The lawyer, in attempting to subject the call to a metaphysics of suspicion ("And who is my neighbor?"), sought to divest the call of concreteness, of reality.

Bonhoeffer realized, however, that "neighborliness is not a quality in other people, it is simply their claim on ourselves. . . . We have literally no time to sit down and ask ourselves whether so-and-so is our neighbor or not. We must get into action and obey — we must behave like a neighbor to him" (COD, 86). Bonhoeffer exemplified *his* obedience to *that* call in Harlem, in his desire to study with Gandhi, and in his opposition to the Aryan clause. For he discovered in himself no impediment to neighborliness. No metaphysics, preconceived and narrow, stood as a barrier that would prevent the sharing of the neighborliness that was first and foremost a blessedness in himself. Costly grace.

"If we despise our brother our worship is unreal, and it forfeits every divine promise. When we come before God with hearts full of contempt and unreconciled with our neighbors, we are, both individually and as a congregation, worshipping an idol" (COD, 144). That is, only the one who truly believes obeys Christ; healthy, sane, holy faith is impossible theoretically. Either one struggles with racism, as if it were the flesh Paul writes about in Romans, or one is *worshiping an idol*.

Who can miss the implications of this for a church that, though on the threshold of war, could not determine who the neighbor was: "Let us . . . as a Church" — wrote Bonhoeffer — "examine ourselves, and see whether we have not often enough wronged our fellow-men. Let us see whether we have tried to win popularity by falling in with the world's hatred, its contempt and its contumely. For if we do that we are murderers" (COD, 144-45).

Always clear to Bonhoeffer, for all intents and purposes, was that the alien I *is* the divine Thou — who one either rejects or accepts. In *The Cost of Discipleship,* Bonhoeffer put it this way: "The Incarnation is the ultimate reason why the service of God cannot be divorced from the service of man" (COD, 145). For Christ — where God and the human life unite — is the center of all that overcomes alienation from others. So the disciple will always stand in commitment to diversity, which Bonhoeffer understood in terms of the Greek word *perisson* — "the *'peculiar'* . . . that which is not 'a matter of course.'" Racism is a matter of course, and the peculiar are those who attain what Bonhoeffer called "'the more,' the 'beyond-all-that'" (COD, 169).

Bonhoeffer made that point when he wrote:

> Where the world seeks gain, the Christian will renounce it. Where the world exploits, he will dispossess himself, and where the world oppresses, he will stoop down and raise up the oppressed. If the world refuses justice, the Christian will pursue mercy, and if the world takes refuge in lies, he will open his mouth for the dumb, and bear testimony to the truth. For the sake of the brother, be he Jew or Greek, bond or free, strong or weak, noble or base, he will renounce all fellowship with the world. (COD, 289)

True humanity (because of the community it nurtures) is but the practice of the neighborliness within one.

The Cost of Discipleship's provocative claim was that any Christian's alienation from the neighbor — and therefore from the cross — was Satan's work. Not the work often thought of in terms of injunctions against drinking and swearing, but precisely that work that prevents Christians from knowing what to do in Nazi-like times. For Bonhoeffer, the Devil was the evil in an apostate church plummeting toward death. That a church refused to suffer meant "that Satan . . . gained entry into the Church . . . trying to tear it away from the cross of its Lord" (COD, 96). Bonhoeffer was ready to suffer, and so could teach his seminarians about the call, the reality, of costly grace.

He showed them that the call to obedience hardly requires persons to deny life's pleasures: human community, hearty repasts, sport, the glories of a beautiful day. Still, he thought that it is only when persons confess Christ's claim on them that they appreciate the benefits of sensual being. It was in that connection that Bonhoeffer wrote, "To endure the cross is not a tragedy; it is the . . . fruit of an exclusive allegiance to Jesus Christ" (COD, 98). The cross, then, has nothing to do with "natural existence" — *natural* meaning "ordinary everyday calamity . . . the trials and tribulations of life." No: the cross "means rejection and shame as well as suffering" — the cross beckons the faithful when genocide springs from the hearts of men (98) The world was on the threshold of a war, a holocaust in the making. Which Christian would follow Jesus? Which Christian would oppose the war and stand against Aryan supremacy? That is the import of Bonhoeffer's famous coinage: "When Christ calls a man he bids him come and die." It is not necessarily a physical death; but in any case a death to business as usual. "In fact," explains Bonhoeffer, "every command of Jesus is a call to die, with all our affections and lusts" (99). And this, writes Bonhoeffer, means "peace and refreshment for the soul" — "the highest joy" (103). Why that is is difficult to explain — that the pain of the victims, and the pain of those who identify with them, is *beatitude.* But it surely has something to do with Bonhoeffer's simple faith before he crossed over: *This is the end, the beginning for me.*

The unwholesome interest in the Other, in terms of the bigotry of the Same, is the sure sign that the meaning of the Beatitude "Blessed are they that mourn, for they shall be comforted" has been missed. Those who mourn are those at the receiving end of racist contempt. Those who mourn, those who carry the heaviest load, are those who are thought to be unworthy of human decency and the right to life. That is, to quote Bonhoeffer: "By 'mourning' Jesus, of course, means doing without what the world calls peace and prosperity." Disciples find they cannot "be in tune with the world or . . . accommodate . . . its standards." Such compromise forsakes God's love that is always betwixt and between I and Thou. It is in that sense that one is to understand Bonhoeffer's claim: "nobody understands his fellow-men better than the Christian fellowship, and that very love impels them to stand aside and mourn" (COD, 121).

Bonhoeffer understood that suffering in terms of another Beatitude: "Blessed are the meek: for they shall inherit the earth." For the "renewal of the earth begins at Golgotha, where the meek One died," and all persons who identify with his meekness know what to do and what has been given them (COD, 123). African-Americans, yesterday as well as today, and the Jews of Holocaust Germany have exemplified such beatitude.

Victims of racism bear insult, as well as injury, daily. This was the case in the Jim Crow South: "When reproached, [blacks held] their peace; when treated with violence they [endured] it patiently; when men [drove] them from their presence, they [yielded] their ground" (COD, 122). To buck such power would have been suicidal, *and* a sure way to undermine the analogy between costly grace and the oppressed. Had the oppressed returned like for like, they would have been divested of much of their nobility; found to be as mean and as Godless as their oppressors.

Nothing satisfies sufferers' craving for freedom except the promise of righteousness, which God gives them at present. "Blessed are they that hunger and thirst for righteousness: for they shall be filled." One filled with that promise understands the costliness of the call to be blessed and therefore shuns the ways of those who think themselves the master race. In understanding, moreover, "Blessed are the merciful: for they shall obtain mercy," disciples — Bonhoeffer explains — have *"renounced their own dignity,* for they are merciful." This was particularly so with Bonhoeffer, who divested himself of pretensions of the bluest eye.

He saw at the root of the anti-Semitism of his time an Aryanness with no dignity apart from the Other. To show genuine mercy was to forego the amenities of an illusory racial purity. To be *called* in the context of the Holocaust was to "have an *irresistible* [emphasis added] love for the down-trodden, the sick, the wretched, the wronged, the outcast and all who are tortured with anxiety" (COD, 124). Merciful Christians rejected the pretensions of the Third Reich. And they *suffered*.

The supralapsarian character of such mercy — i.e., Bonhoeffer's implication that the love for the wronged is irresistible — attests to his understanding of the Beatitude "Blessed are the pure in heart: for they shall see God." To be called is to act (to know what to do); to have seen, to have been in the real presence of Jesus — in the sense of *actus directus* (and in the sense of knowing what has been given). Christ himself occasions such purity in the one who is called: "Only they will see God," explained Bonhoeffer, "who in this life have looked solely unto Jesus Christ, the Son of God" (COD, 126).

The sight could not have been a pretty one: The sight of a broken and humiliated savior is a heavy load; so heavy as to cause one to identify with the Jews, and in the name of the One who was himself a Jew. Bonhoeffer realized his church did not want that kind of Lord ("a suffering messiah"); for "the Church of Christ . . . does not like to have the law of suffering imposed on it by its Lord" (COD, 96). Only those who *see* him overcome the racism that destroys the neighbor. "For then their hearts are free from all defiling phantasies and . . . not distracted by conflicting desires and intentions." Called-ones, alone, are pure in heart, are "a reflection of the image of Jesus Christ" (126).

Only the pure in heart can live out the meaning of this Beatitude: "Blessed are the peacemakers: for they shall be called the children of God." Bonhoeffer realized that war is never far behind waxing racist sentiment; which underlines the value of the final two Beatitudes. "Blessed are they that have been persecuted for righteousness' sake: for theirs is the kingdom of heaven"; and "Blessed are you when men shall reproach you, and persecute you, and say all manner of evil against you falsely for my sake. Rejoice and be exceeding glad, for great is your reward in heaven: for so persecuted they the prophets which were before you."

Bonhoeffer argued that those who did not experience the costliness of God's righteousness, and incur the calumny of the Godless, were no longer the salt of the earth — "salt, the most indispensable necessity of life." The earth itself attains fecundity because of this salt; and Bonhoeffer considered the salt of the earth to be "the poor, ignoble and weak, whom the world rejects" (COD, 129). The world's rejection of them is the sign of the world's demise, for to reject the salt of the earth is to set upon the path of destruction.

That Jesus said you *are* the salt of the earth was significant for Bonhoeffer; "Jesus does not say: 'You *must* be the salt,'" as if the blessedness of "saltiness" were self-bestowed. Salt, argued Bonhoeffer, is "said to be imperishable; it can never lose its cleansing properties." Salt is thus a metaphor for the irresistibility of costly grace: The problem of racist enmity is so deeply entrenched in human existence that none who recognizes it as sin and death thinks of such grace as a self-possessed virtue. "Again," explained Bonhoeffer, "it is: 'Ye *are* the salt,' not ye *have* the salt" (COD, 130). (Salt is to discipleship as grace is to election.) Bonhoeffer's claim that salt may lose its properties — "lose its savor and cease to be salt at all" — appears to contradict what he has said regarding salt's indomitable-ness. But his point is that "we are the salt of the earth, or else we are annihilated; either we follow the call or we are crushed beneath it" (131).

Complementing the salt metaphor in *The Cost of Discipleship* is the metaphor of light: The salt of the earth are far in advance of all others, and so they let their light shine with irrepressible conviction. Jesus's call, "You *are* the light of the world," means that costly grace is indelible. His "followers are a visible community; their discipleship visible in action which lifts them out of the world — otherwise it would not be discipleship." Indelible, costly grace "is as visible to the world as a light in the darkness or a mountain rising from a plain" (132).

Bonhoeffer's critics derided his insights as *illuminisme (Schwärmen),* a species of gnosticism as it were. Although he eschewed the "rusty swords" of the pathetic want-to-be knight *Don Quixote,* Bonhoeffer appeared quixotic to those who found him *too* evangelical. Prepared to pay the price for that, he argued that none who go against the stream to such an extent as to cut a tragic-comic figure have made *themselves* such individuals: "it is Christ who makes them individuals by calling them" (COD, 105). Bonhoeffer's individuality took shape in his rejection of what he called "'Reformation theology' which boldly claims the name of *theologia crucis,* and pretends to prefer to Pharisaic ostentation a modest invisibility, which in practice means conformity to the world" (132).

To quote Bonhoeffer, moreover: "Every [one] is called separately, and must follow alone. But [certain individuals] are frightened of solitude, and they try to protect themselves from it by merging themselves in the *society* of their fellow-men and in their material environment" (COD, 105, emphasis added). Bonhoeffer, though, had looked on Jesus — at least one tends to think that he had — and so realized that the call to obedience — to incontrovertible otherness — mandated that persons step from the milieu of a sameness so overgrown with a racist ethic, and a racist religion, and a racist metaphysics.

It was exactly his rejection of such illusion that isolated him. As of 1940, he was forbidden to publish, to speak in public, and had to inform the police of his whereabouts (Dumas 1968, 71-72). For he had heard the call: *When Christ calls a man he bids him come and die.* So Bonhoeffer said goodbye to his role as minister, seminary head, and up-and-coming scholar. He, alone, took on the risk of clandestine work against the Nazi regime. Traveling to Switzerland, Norway, and Sweden — trying to drum up Allied support — he put his life in danger, all the more so because he worked to get Jews out of the country. All of that heroism is owed to Bonhoeffer's insight regarding what happens to persons when they are willing "to stand alone before Jesus and to be compelled to decide with their eyes fixed on him alone." This *actus directus* is such that "neither father nor mother, neither wife nor child, neither nationality nor tradition, can protect a man at the moment of his call" (COD, 105).

III
Ethics

Bonhoeffer wrote his *Ethics* during the time he was involved in counterespionage (he hid portions of the book, which is but a collection of fragments, in unlikely places). He makes it clear that nothing is as much of an impediment to discipleship as *conscience* — "the voice of apostate life which desires . . . to remain one with itself." The prison of the Same, conscience believes that it is "identical with good, and . . . does not register the fact, that even in this, man is in a state of disunion with his origin" (E, 24). "What God had given [us] to be" is surrendered to a false autonomy based on the distinction between relative good and relative evil, which are adjudicated by persons trapped in the cul-de-sac of playing god — "a god against God" (18-19).

In "forbidden actions," conscience "sees a peril to life as a whole, that is to say, disunion with oneself; it recalls what is long past and represents this disunion as something which is already accomplished and irreparable, but the final criterion remains precisely that unity with oneself which is imperilled only in the particular instance in which the prohibition is disobeyed" (E, 24). Somewhere inside the one who stops shy of transgressing such prohibition is the memory of the fall — "this disunion as something . . . already accomplished and irreparable." For regardless of how one accounts for it, people are prone to self-destruction. But few see that "conscience does not, like shame, embrace the whole of life." For most, then, the sense of what-is-forbidden-and-what-is-not is exceedingly narrow.

What is forbidden is contact — indirect contact — with the Other. What is permitted is the interaction of the Same; and the great blind spot is the *shame* of it. The killing of Jews and the occupation of lands belonging to others was judged, by dint of conscience, to be ethical for the sake of the master race. The racists of Bonhoeffer's time forced their swastika onto Europe, forcing world war, promoting death and *shame,* shame racists cannot see, and thus cannot overcome. For "shame is overcome only in the enduring of an act of final shaming, namely the becoming manifest of knowledge before God. . . . Shame is overcome only in the shaming through the forgiveness of sin . . . through the restoration of fellowship with God and other [people]" (E, 23).

Bonhoeffer, then, found the remedy to shame — which sets the human race against itself to the extent that shame is covered up by dint of conscience — to be simple: Love God and the neighbor as thyself. As he argued in *The Cost of Discipleship,* he also argues in *Ethics* that love, though costly, begins with each individual — a beginning stripped bare of judgment, unencumbered therefore by racist metaphysics, that grants to the Thou the freedom to reciprocate the "will of God," which "established the freedom and the simplicity of all action" (E, 30).

Bonhoeffer knew what to do: He saw "the black storm-cloud and the brilliant lighting-flash," rather than "the uniform greyness of the rainy day." He joined the conspiracy out of the realization that the true Christian and the Godless villain are not theoretical constructs. They are *real:* "They emerge from primeval depths and by their appearance they tear open the infernal or the divine abyss from which they come and enable us to see for a moment into mysteries of which we had never dreamed." In such a time, any Christian worth his salt had to know, "What is worse than doing evil is being evil": better to break from clergy ethics than to have complicity in the workings of the death camps (E, 64). Hitler had to be stopped by any means necessary. As Bonhoeffer saw it, Hitler rejected the "rich and manifold variety of God's creation." The distinctions within the human race are all too apparent, however, for one to force them into "the false uniformity or . . . pattern of an ideal or a type or a definite picture of the human character."

"To be conformed with the Incarnate," wrote Bonhoeffer, moreover, "is to be a real [person]." "The quest for the superman . . . the pursuit of the heroic, the cult of the demigod . . . is untrue." In that critique of Nazi paganism, Bonhoeffer makes it clear, once more, that sameness, uniformity, is chimera. Diversity, manifold otherness, is reality. For "to be conformed with the Incarnate is to have the right to be the [person] one really is." Within such diversity each is permitted to be him or herself, which quells pretense, hypocrisy, delusion, and, therefore, the deception whereby people cling to a metaphysical concept of humanity — "something other, better and more ideal than what one is." "God loves the real man. God became a real man" (E, 81).

Bonhoeffer thought no Western nation could afford to ignore German idolatry because "the form of Christ [was] the unity of the Western nations" (E, 87). Bonhoeffer succumbed here to a Western chauvinism that credits historical consciousness to Europe alone. He thought Asia locked in a Hindu-like "timelessness" or a Japanese-style ancestor deification, and mentioned Africa not at all (88). One wonders how to weigh that, as Bonhoeffer argued on other occasions that the West was too decadent to be trusted with the Christian heritage. He makes it clear, however, that history has to do with humiliation and suffering, not the apotheosis of European culture and consciousness. Certainly, Bonhoeffer thought God had chosen the West — but not in any sense that escaped formation in costly grace (89). *The form of Christ* — the costliness of grace — had to do with the Jews:

> An expulsion of the Jews from the West must necessarily bring with it the expulsion of Christ. For Jesus Christ was a Jew. (E, 90)

Bonhoeffer found that Hellenism was at the root of Germany's hostility to Christ, and therefore at the root of the hostility to the Jews. The rest of Europe had "sought in antiquity mainly for the Roman heritage," but the Germans had been "determined primarily by Hellenism" (90). Bonhoeffer, in fact, thought the Reformation, and the attendant rise of German nationalism, birthed the spirit of the Enlightenment and thus the love for Greek antiquity, the symbol of which was Nietzsche. ("It was only from the soil of the German Reformation that there could spring a Nietzsche," wrote Bonhoeffer.)

Germany, as he saw it, had reverted to its "Germanic, pre-Christian ethnic past." And who misses the fact that the Aryan ideal was the likeness of a Greek god. Because Germany favored that ideal to Christ (a Jew), there was no real appeal to German history — only an "indigenous pre-Christian past [that went] hand in hand with a mythologization of history" (E, 92). He reminded his countrymen, "Our forefathers are for us not ancestors who are made the object of worship and veneration. Interest in genealogies can all too easily become mythologization" (89). Shame: With Luther himself reduced to a pagan entity, but moreover with faith in God but a shibboleth for jingoism, "all that remained was a rationalized and mechanized world" (96).

That world — *rationalized, secularized* — first took root "in Catholic France" (E, 97). The French Revolution "emancipated reason" — the reigning "efflorescence of the rational and empirical sciences" at work in today's *monde majeure.* Unlike a less modern time, when technology, sprung from artisanship, served human beings and complemented the environment, modern technology, crassly functional, enslaved human beings and was nature's nemesis. (Picture, for example, the gun as the symbol of this modernity, particularly where racial cleansing — *à la* Bosnia and Rwanda — is concerned.) For Bonhoeffer, the French Revolution was a major factor in causing such technology to gain the upper hand, especially as it unleashed the masses, who were both victims and perpetrators of modernity, the metonym of which is the machine — "the violation and exploitation of nature" (98).

The liberty the Revolution brought — the rise of the bourgeoisie and "the dark menace of the masses" — was in truth an antiliberty for Bonhoeffer. For the unlettered and uncouth masses made "their own law, the law of misery . . . a violent law, and short-lived." Bonhoeffer thought that the Nazi war was "the culmination and crisis of [that] uprising" (E, 100). That is, one of the things the Revolution engendered was nationalism (a "new unity"), which led "inevitably to war." Bonhoeffer wrote:

The new unity which the French Revolution brought to Europe — and what we are experiencing today is the crisis of this unity — is therefore western godlessness. It is totally different from the atheism of certain individual Greek, Indian, Chinese and western thinkers. It is not the theoretical denial of the existence of God. It is itself a religion, a religion of hostility to God. . . . Its god is the New Man, no matter whether he bears the trademark of Bolshevism or of Christianity. This differs fundamentally from all paganism, for in paganism gods are adored in the form of men but here it is man who is adored in the form of God, indeed in the form of Jesus Christ. (102-3)

One might say that this New Man has led the world to the brink of what Bonhoeffer called the void, toward which he saw the Western world drifting — "a specifically western void, a rebellious and outrageous void . . . which is the enemy of God and man. . . . It is a creative void, which blows its anti-god's breath into the nostrils of all that is established and awakens it to a false semblance of new life while sucking out from it its proper essence, until at last it falls in ruin as a lifeless husk and is cast away" (E, 105-6).

An "apostasy from all that is established," the West, led by the New Man, had become barren; the Holocaust, its *lifeless husk*. Bonhoeffer believed that the churches, alone — "guardians of the heritage of the Middle Ages and of the Reformation and especially as witnesses of the miracle of God in Jesus Christ" — could rescue persons from the *void*. The churches were to be helped in this by the "restrainer," the state — "that is to say the remaining force of order which still opposes effective resistance to the process of decay" (E, 108). Bonhoeffer's hope was that he and his fellow conspirators would eliminate Hitler, returning Germany to the integrity of its historical heritage: the church as *Christ existing as community,* and the state as the authority over the mob.

Church and state are integral to Bonhoeffer's sense of the penultimate and the ultimate. By the penultimate Bonhoeffer means, at least, the "natural," which is the world sustained by God, who gives the ultimate gift — justification by faith alone — which makes life possible for Christ's sake. For God-in-Christ redeems the world by way of his body, the church; which may work in conjunction with

150

the state. Providential — in that it is something rather than nothing — the natural is "the safeguarding of life against the unnatural [which was sheer enmity toward the cross for Bonhoeffer]. It is in the last analysis life itself that tends towards the natural and keeps turning against the unnatural and bringing about its downfall" (E, 147).

Natural-persons, who are Christian, respond to the call to costly grace but do not succumb to radicalism on the one hand or compromise on the other. Thinking itself the ultimate — remember the Grand Inquisitor? — *radicalism* destroys the penultimate hallowed by Christ. ("But devils are not cast out through Beelzebub.") Sprung from hostility to the ultimate, *compromise* capitulates to forces that abuse the penultimate hallowed by Christ. (Adaptability, "even to the point of resignedness, and mere worldly-wise prudence and discretion are passed off as genuine openness to the world and as genuine Christian charity.")

Born from an arrogance that deigns to improve upon the natural, radicalism hates the real. Born from a sloth that capitulates to the unnatural, compromise hates the Christ. Both are hostile to Christ, in fact (129-30). And both bring out the horror of racism as they pertain to the reality that moved Bonhoeffer to pen his *Ethics*. Nazi Christians were radicals, who hated the penultimate as well as the ultimate; those who gave in to them, in order to protect the church, hated the ultimate as well as the penultimate. Radicals and compromisers both were blind to Christ — "In Him alone lies the solution for the problem of the relation between the ultimate and the penultimate" (130).

Bonhoeffer avoids two other extremes — "vitalism" and "the mechanization of life." Vitalism so glorifies the natural as to lose sight of humanity's fallenness, positing "itself as an absolute, as an end in itself." The mechanization of life so crushes diversity as to deify "some higher institution or organization" — the collectivity — completing the idolatry that began with vitalism. That is, "The collectivity is the god to whom individual and social life are sacrificed in the process of their total mechanization" (150).

151

One sees this vitalism and mechanization of life in terms of the uniformity of the Nazi war machine, well-oiled, spreading devastation throughout Europe. What Bonhoeffer called "the rights of natural life" were for a time extinguished for millions by the formidable love of what is unnatural. Life gave way to death; which is always the case when racist values become so vitalistic as to become mechanized, always the case when reverence of the Other ceases to be the way of the natural life.

Bonhoeffer sums up the import of the natural life in terms of the Latin idiom *suum cuique* — "to each his own":

> This principle expresses not only the multiplicity of the natural and of the rights that pertain to it but also the unity which the right retains even in this multiplicity. The principle is misapplied whenever there is a violation of either the multiplicity or the unity of the rights . . . given with the natural. This is the case if "his own" is taken to mean "the *same,*" so that the manifoldness of the natural is destroyed in favor of an abstract law, and it is also the case if "his own" is defined arbitrarily and subjectively so that the unity of rights is nullified in the interests of free self-will. (E, 152, emphasis added).

This is the case if "his own" is taken to mean "the same*," so that the manifoldness of the natural is destroyed in favor of an abstract law, and it is also the case if "his own" is defined arbitrarily and subjectively so that the unity of rights is nullified in the interests of free self-will* — such racism was the leitmotif of Hitler's *Mein Kampf.*

"No more than Nature desires the mating of weaker with stronger individuals," wrote Hitler, "even less does she desire the blending of a higher with a lower race, since, if she did, her whole work of higher breeding, over hundreds of thousands of years, might be ruined with one blow" (Hitler 1971, 286). Suffice it to say the higher race was the Aryan — "He is the Prometheus of mankind from whose bright forehead the divine spark of genius has sprung at all times, forever kindling anew that fire of knowledge which illumined the night of silent mysteries and thus caused man to climb the path to mastery over the other beings of the earth" (290). To Hitler, then, *to each his own* meant no "racial crossing"; for "to bring about such a development [was] . . . nothing else but to sin against the will of the eternal creator" (286).

For Bonhoeffer it is also true that "due honor is . . . rendered to the will and to the gift of the Creator," when *to each is own* is upheld; but in the sense that individuals are compelled to look to other individuals as inviolate alien I's. Hitler's focus on race, however, entailed the concession of a "natural right only to the community and not to the individual" (E, 153). *Individuals* were destroyed for the sake of a community misconstrued on the basis of sameness.

God, however, willed "to create the individual and to endow him with eternal life." What *right,* then, had bigots to extinguish what God created inextinguishable? For "the principle of *suum cuique* is . . . in accord with reality and . . . within the natural life, discerns the right which is given to the individual by God" (E, 154). "And where if not in God should there lie the criterion for the ultimate value of a life?" (163).

What right did racists have to prohibit miscegenation (a meaningless word insofar as it caters to the illusion that there are races as opposed to *the* human race)? Part of Hitler's war agenda was to guarantee that marriages between Aryans would hold sway in the world:

> Blood mixture and the resultant drop in the racial level is the sole cause of the dying out of old cultures; for men do not perish as a result of lost wars, but by the loss of that force of resistance which is continued only in pure blood. All who are not of good race in this world are chaff. (Hitler 1971, 296)

Hitler held that miscegenation must be stopped "by raising marriage from the level of a continuous defilement of the race, and give it the consecration of an institution which is called upon to produce images of the Lord and not monstrosities halfway between man and ape" (402).

Bonhoeffer saw that for what it was — a death wish: "an arbitrary diminution of the abundance of marriage and consequently also of the propagation of the human race which God desires." According to Bonhoeffer:

> Alien authorities assert a claim to direct and shape the coming generation, and they thereby impoverish the abundance of God's creation which seeks to develop through the desire of individuals for children of their own and not through the compulsory breeding of a particular human type. This constitutes a disastrous interference in the natural order of the world. Concerned as they are for the securing of new blood for their . . . nation, and possessing very little confidence in natural inhibitions and natural choice, they deliberately deprive themselves of unsuspected human forces. (E, 174-75)

Nazi marriages, *the compulsory breeding of a particular human type,* diminished human possibilities in undermining the oneness of the human race and forbidding the newness that would embellish and enrich human diversity.

A fragment of the *Ethics,* which Bethge footnotes, suggests, moreover, that such racism is fundamentally uncultured. Culture, Bonhoeffer suggests, comprises an openness to the Other, an embracing of "the *whole* of natural and mental existence (without specialization)." A cultured person appreciates all things that express human creativity. The illusion that culture is vital and sublime only if it conforms to a European ethos is gauche.

In that regard, Bonhoeffer notes the boorishness of those prone to ridicule African people as if they were below the Europeans — for he wrote: "It is uncultured to laugh at a film when Negro dances are performed. . . . It is uncultured to ridicule something merely because it is different from oneself" (E,187). The movie Bonhoeffer had in mind is a mystery to me — one depicting blacks' dances, *à la*

Harlem's Cotton Club, or snatches of African dance in *Tarzan?* But during the height of the Nazi period, African people were dubbed by Hitler as little more than "primitive and inferior."

To be called by Christ is to be responsible for and free in regard to the neighbor; who, for Bonhoeffer — reiterating his discussion of neighborliness in *The Cost of Discipleship* — is never the neighbor in the vulgar sense of the word. The neighbor could be a world away — across the Atlantic, in the United States. Indeed, referring to the case of the Scottsboro boys, Bonhoeffer wrote:

> My neighbor may well be one who is extremely remote from me, and one who is extremely remote from me may well be my neighbor. By a terrible miscarriage of justice in the United States in 1[9]31 nine young Negroes, whose guilt could not be proved, were sentenced to death for the rape of a white girl of doubtful reputation. There arose a storm of indignation which found expression in open letters from some of the most authoritative public figures in Europe. A Christian who was perturbed by this affair asked a prominent cleric in Germany whether he, too, ought not raise his voice in this matter, and on the grounds of the "Lutheran" idea of vocation, that is to say, on the grounds of the limitation of his responsibility, the clergyman refused. (E, 260)

Having had but a narrow neighborliness within himself — for he later revised his judgment — the prominent cleric did not have at first "the openness of the commandment of brotherly love in the face of any false limitation" and did not "safeguard the concept of vocation in the liberty with which the gospel invests it" (261). Failing to embrace the freedom that is born from unqualified responsibility toward the Other, failing to "keep open the boundary," the pastor made sameness into an ethic.

That one's responsibility toward his or her neighbor is a far-reaching responsibility is a claim related to Bonhoeffer's seemingly elitist assertion: "We can no longer escape the fact that the ethical calls for clear relationships in terms of superiority and inferiority. . . . Superiority does not consist in the subjective values of the superior man, but it derives its legitimation from a concrete objective commission" (E, 274). Such a commission is integral to the mandates — *marriage, labor, government, church* — which were instituted by God and gave meaning and form to the natural (the penultimate). Their divine (ultimate) import is to be seen solely in relation to Christ. The superior is upheld by Christ. By superiority, then, Bonhoeffer does not mean the vulgar priority of one class or caste over another.

By inferiority, Bonhoeffer means at least two things. First, inferiority refers to those who adhere to the mandates and are obedient to Christ. Second, inferiority means a racist orientation — "armed with the dark forces of destruction, denial, doubt and rebellion" — which flourished when the Führer became the Lord. His *Mein Kampf* makes this point in terms of "folkish philosophy," which

> by no means believes in the equality of races, but along with their difference it recognizes their higher or lesser value and feels obligated, through this knowledge, to promote the victory of the better and stronger with the eternal will that dominates the universe. . . . It believes in the necessity of an idealization of humanity, in which alone it sees the premise for the existence of humanity. . . . But it cannot grant the right to existence even to an ethical idea if this idea represents a danger for the racial life of the bearers of a higher ethics; for in a bastardized and niggerized world all the concepts of the humanly beautiful and sublime, as well as all ideas of an idealized future of our humanity, would be lost forever. (Hitler 1971, 383)

In the context of the genocide of the Jews, someone had to rise above the sickness and say — but moreover *do* — something that had the effect of revealing nazism as the *inferior* blight that it was. Not because this someone was in himself *superior*, but because God had called him or her to neighborliness. One was called to see that "the only possible object of a 'Christian ethic,' an object which lies beyond the 'ethical,'" was God's commandment.

"The commandment of God is the total and concrete claim laid to [us] by the merciful and holy God in Jesus Christ" (E, 277). To see Jesus — and really see him — is to live in a way that requires no ethical admonition. For:

> The commandment of God becomes the element in which one lives without always being conscious of it, and, thus it implies freedom of movement and of action, freedom from the fear of decision, freedom from fear to act, it implies certainty, quietude, confidence, balance and peace. I honor my parents, I am faithful in marriage, I respect the lives and property of others, not because at the frontiers of my life there is a threatening "thou shalt not," but because I accept as holy institutions of God these realities, parents, marriage, life and property, which confront me in the midst and in the fullness of life. (280-81)

Under the superior mandates, life is a gift — the free and gracious enjoyment of I and Thou.

Ethics "can only wish to keep interrupting this life, confronting it at every moment with nothing but the conflict of duties" (E, 282). Ethics in "race" relations, then, arise only where there is the illusion of racialist metaphysics (*à la Mein Kampf*). Those free of such metaphysics — the extraordinary — live unencumbered by "Thou shalt *not!*" They — disciples — extend the neighborliness within them to the Other. In communion with others, such individuals know what to do when crises emerge. They teach others that the "'ethical' defines only the boundary, the formal and the negative, and is therefore possible as a theme only on the periphery, formally and negatively" (284). On the periphery — called by costly grace — these extraordinary ones obey Christ.

"The purpose and aim of the dominion of Christ," writes Bonhoeffer, "is not to make the worldly order godly or to subordinate it to the Church but to set it free for true worldliness" (E, 328-29).

157

True worldliness and racism are at odds: Racism rejects Jesus' authority, retreats from reality. And when racism becomes necrophilic, as it did in the hands of the Nazis, the burden of obedience to Christ is heavy indeed. For any state in which the *government* fails to administer justice, fails to nurture both the family *(marriage)* and *labor,* and any *church* that fails to proclaim a God who is no respecter of persons — are a state and a church to be opposed, for Christ's sake!

To the extent that ethics enable one to stand up for his or her neighbors, knowing what to do *is* redemptive — even if such redemption weighs upon one as heavily as it did upon Bonhoeffer. A heavy load: Bonhoeffer paid the penultimate price. One has the hope that his faith abides. By and By.

> O Christians, can't you rise and tell,
> I'm going to lay down this heavy load,
> That Jesus hath done all things well,
> I'm going to lay down this heavy load.

CHAPTER 5

There's Room for Many a More: Bonhoeffer's Legacy for the Twenty-first Century

The Gospel train's a-coming, I hear it just at hand,
I hear the car wheels rumbling, and rolling through the land.
I hear the train a-coming, she's coming round the curve,
She's loosened all her steam and brakes, and straining every nerve.
The fare is cheap and all can go, the rich and poor are there,
No second class aboard this train, no difference in the fare.

"Get on board little children/get on board little children/get on board little children/ — there's room for many a more." So goes "The Gospel Train's" refrain, which sums up, I think, Bonhoeffer's hope even as he faced his final moments at Flossenbürg: The whole world is in God's hands, and all persons, no matter their color or their ethnicity, belong to God, who is no respecter of persons. All are welcome where God is, and none can stop the power of God, who means for all people to be free. *The fare is cheap and all can go, the rich and poor are there.*

Still, the juxtaposition is curious: a God whose power is weakness, as reflected in Bonhoeffer's hanging; and the slaves' image of God's authority — a mighty, unstoppable train moving full steam ahead. How *does* one reconcile such disparate images? Only in realizing that they both portray a God who defeats evil in falling victim to it. That is certainly a matter of faith.

Ostensibly, the slaves who sang "The Gospel Train" had no ground to sing as they did. Bonhoeffer had no ground to say just before he was executed, *This is the end — for me the beginning of life.* The only thing squarely beneath their feet was their suffering — suffering at the hands of racists, suffering that, in itself, neither accounted for the slaves' *no second class aboard this train, no difference in the fare,* nor condemned Bonhoeffer's beatitude. Their appeal was to evidence unseen, which hardly made their trials easier for them to take.

That, according to Bonhoeffer, was as it should have been: "The Christian has no last line of escape . . . from earthly tasks and difficulties into the eternal, but, like Christ himself ('My God, why hast thou forsaken me?') . . . must drink the earthly cup to the dregs" (LPP, 337). Without turning whatever misery comes their way into a fetish, without reveling in a religious preoccupation with sin, which saps life of its wholesome potential, true Christians face the world without illusion, refusing to deform their faith into a religious crutch. They are religionless and therefore godless — their way to God is through a human being, who was not himself a god, but a Jew who received no reprieve from the challenges and the horrors of life. That is, Christ is not "an object of religion, but something quite different, really the Lord of the world" (LPP, 281).

According to Bethge, Bonhoeffer meant six things by religion during his incarceration: (1) metaphysics; (2) individualism; (3) partiality; (4) the deus ex machina; (5) tutelage; and (6) dispensability.

Metaphysics, a grand form of solipsism, bifurcates heaven and earth in banishing God to an otherworldly domain that is the object of "religious longing": "Supernatural and mythological formulations obscure the direct immediacy of the Gospel, and the exotic nature of the context in which it is presented has nothing to do with the message itself" (Bethge 1985, 777). One forsakes the world as well as the gospel for the ghetto of the mind. *Individualism* forsakes community — forsakes the world — in the preoccupation with one's private life. Whatever God there is is the God of one's soul — to such an extent that the call to neighborliness is repelled by the inner sanctum (provincial and disingenuous) of the "pious." Bonhoeffer, then, "was sensitive to the tendency to direct one's gaze to the private sphere of man and cultivate the 'salvation of one's own soul' at the cost of the world and the *familia Dei*" (778).

Partiality forsakes the world through a narrow focus on whatever is thought to be the province of religion — Seeburg's religious a priori, for instance, or Schleiermacher's feeling. Partiality also forfeits wholeness in the preoccupation with whatever is unknown and unexplored (namely what has not been discredited by the enlightened mind). The call to *serve* the world *as it is* is unheeded. "The fatal thing is that here religion directs all interest towards its frontiers and, institutionalized, keeps watch over them" — a church with its head buried in the sand. The *deus ex machina,* the stop-gap god (the god of the gaps), is a deity one concocts as a means of escaping life's challenges and horrors. "This idea again makes religion an escape from real life and from mature responsibility for it" (Bethge 1985, 779).

One beholden to *privilege* falsely assumes that he is better than others, who are, ostensibly, the nonelect. A smoke screen for bigotry, privilege — remember this quote from chapter one — "has presided over a vast number of acts of violence throughout history: Christians against non-Christians, theists against atheists, or whites against colored people" (Bethge 1985, 780). *Tutelage* deigns to show the world the way to "truth" — which is but the illusion of the encapsulated self. Finally, *dispensability* is the sure sense that all of that conditioned by Western religiousness (metaphysics, individualism, et cetera) is expendable — a bygone relic that is irrelevant in the *monde majeure.*

Bonhoeffer's rejection of religion boiled down to one thing — a certain *actus directus.* For one must recognize

161

not only the presence, but also the person of Jesus. The basic thing is always simply him and the way he is present to us: 1. he, Jesus, does not call for any acceptance of preliminary systems of thought and behavior; 2. he is anti-individualist, and, in a totally exposed and unprotected way, the man for others; 3. he does not pray as if he made part payment by installments, but with his life; 4. he turns away from the temptation of the *deus ex machina;* 5. he turns away from the privileged classes and sits down with the outcasts; and 6. he liberates [persons] to find their own responsible answer to life through his own powerlessness, which is both shaming and utterly convincing. (Bethge 1985, 781)

More than anything else, Bonhoeffer's religionlessness pondered God's weakness in the world; for Christ *liberates [persons] to find their own responsible answer to life through his own powerlessness, which is both shaming and utterly convincing.* Matthew 8:17 — "That it might be fulfilled which was spoken by Isaiah the prophet, saying, he took our infirmities, and bore our sickness" — is what Bonhoeffer had in mind. For "the Bible," wrote Bonhoeffer, "directs [us] to God's powerlessness and suffering; *only the suffering God can help*" (LPP, 361; emphasis added).

Bonhoeffer's nonreligious question is "What do a church, a community, a sermon, a liturgy, a Christian life mean in a religionless world? How do we speak of God — without religion, i.e. without the temporally conditioned presuppositions of metaphysics, inwardness, and so on?" (LPP, 280). The Enlightenment had so undermined a medieval style of piety, as well as archaic philosophies, that the world — meaning an *epoch,* with its engines and skyscrapers, and knowledge — had little use for religion.

Religious people are out of touch with reality. Bonhoeffer was "reluctant to mention God by name to religious people"; and would really "dry up almost completely and feel awkward" when persons actually began "to talk in religious jargon" (LPP, 281). He envisioned an openness to God beyond the "virgin birth, Trinity, or anything else" — beyond the *actus reflexus* (the *old time religion*), that pointed the way forward to costly grace. It was not enough for him to take refuge in these symbols. Better to weigh them as guides for living; as truths to be assimilated in concert with life's very real ups and downs, not as things to be swallowed lock stock and barrel (286). Far more important than doctrine is "prayer and righteous action among" persons (300). *The fare is cheap and all can go . . .*

Another spiritual also makes the point, I think:

> Never seen the like since I been born,
> The people keep a-coming,
> and the train done gone.

The people kept coming to the inn where Jesus' mother had been denied a room. But Jesus had already been born in a manger. The people were too late, out of step with the way God was working. And the meaning of that story is: religious people, content to mouth the *actus reflexus* of the church, do not see — *the train done gone!* How out of step with the times, then — *Never seen the like since I been born!* — is a racist enclave that calls itself a church.

To be sure, "The Gospel Train" provides a clue to what Bonhoeffer envisioned — "a new language, perhaps quite non-religious, but liberating and redeeming — as was Jesus' language — [that] will shock people and yet overcome them by its power . . . the language of a new righteousness and truth, proclaiming God's peace . . . and the coming . . . kingdom" (LPP, 300). *No second class aboard this train, no difference in the fare.*

How wrong Hitler was. For if faith itself refuses to deny the world in seeking the *living* Christ, who is far more dynamic than yesterday's formulas can render him, if faith is religionless in that sense — how far from reality Hitler's folkish concept was! Inspired by Wagner's operas, that set the legends of ancient, Viking-like ancestors — Siegfried, Kriemhild, Brunhild, Hagen — to music, the folkish concept was steeped in mythology. Folklore about dragons, conquest, fighting gods, and invincible champions defined a xenophobic Germany, which came to see in Hitler the reincarnation of its origins — the deification of itself.

The National Reich Church of Germany was to enshrine this religion, as was made clear by its thirty articles, two of which stated:

> 19. On the altars there must be nothing but *Mein Kampf* (to the German nation and therefore to God the most sacred book) and to the left of the altar a sword.

> 30. On the day of its foundation, the Christian Cross must be removed from all churches, cathedrals and chapels . . . and it must be superseded by the only unconquerable symbol, the swastika. (Shirer 1992, 332-33)

The religionless truth, however, is *no second class aboard this train*.

Bonhoeffer's disdain for a person who said something uncultured about the Jews brings that to light: *no difference in the fare*. While in prison, Bonhoeffer wrote to his niece (Renate) and her husband (Bethge):

> I've had to take a new line with the companion of my daily walks. Although he has done his best to ingratiate himself with me, he let fall a remark about the *Gert* [emphasis added] problem, etc., lately that has made me more cool to him than I have ever been to anyone before; I've also arranged for him to be deprived promptly of all little comforts. Now he feels obliged to go round whimpering for a time, but it leaves me — I am surprised myself, but interested too — absolutely cold. He really is a pitiful figure, but certainly not "poor Lazarus." (LPP, 194-95)

Lazarus was indigent and diseased, the antithesis of the rich man who snubbed him. But Lazarus goes to heaven — *was carried by the angels to Abraham's bosom* (Lk 16:22). The rich man goes to his damnation.

The racist, who *let fall a remark about the* Gert *problem,* was pitiful in the sense that the rich man was — quite out of touch with reality.

For God is far closer to a poor man full of sores than to a rich *man clothed in purple and fine linen and who feasted sumptuously everyday.* The anti-Semite was to the Jews as the rich man was to Lazarus. And so, the racist sharpened Bonhoeffer's identity as a man of faith, a lover of the spirituals:

> . . . Poor man Lazarus, poor as I,
> When he died he found a home on high,
> He had a home in that rock,
> Don't you see?

That he had *a home in that rock* was, beyond doubt, Bonhoeffer's bottom line — his *cantus firmus.*

The significance of this *cantus firmus* is found in a letter Bonhoeffer wrote to Eberhard Bethge, who had written Bonhoeffer about the trials of war. Writing back to his buddy, Bonhoeffer said: "If a man loves he wants to live, to live above all, and hates everything that represents a threat to his life." In a time of war and the Holocaust, nearly everything seemed to threaten life and put an end to love. It was enough to drive a man mad — the thought of never being with one's beloved again. Bonhoeffer's advice was for Bethge to keep to the bottom line:

> What I mean is that God wants us to love him eternally with our hearts — not in such a way as to injure or weaken our earthly love, but to provide a kind of *cantus firmus* to which other melodies of life provide the counterpoint. . . . Do you see what I'm driving at? I wanted to tell you to have a good, clear *cantus firmus;* that is the only way to a full and perfect sound, when the counterpoint has a firm support and can't come adrift or get out of tune, while remaining a distinct whole in its own right. (LPP, 302-3)

The racist had no clue as to the relation of this *cantus firmus* — *Get on board little children/get on board little children . . .* — to Franz, to Gerhard, to Sabine. Bonhoeffer had no time for him.

What does all that — a sixfold religionlessness; the suffering God; the limitations of doctrine, anti-Semitism — mean for the twenty-first century? From his cell, Bonhoeffer observed that "false developments and failures do not make the world doubt the necessity of the course that it is taking, or of its development; they are accepted with fortitude and detachment as part of the bargain" (LPP, 326). And so it is today: If World War II, with its Holocaust, did not shake the myth of progress to its foundations, surely the proliferating crises in Africa — holocaust after holocaust after holocaust — do not. Neither do the holocausts in Eastern Europe (Bosnia) and in Central America (Guatemala). Those horrors are thought to be par for the course, the inevitable costs of a world on the move from what it was. But a course to where in the twenty-first century?

If the meaning of Bonhoeffer's religionlessness is concentrated in his *only the suffering God can help,* and in his view that one is *summoned to share in God's suffering at the hands of a [G]odless world* — is it not so that we, on the threshold of the twenty-first century, learn to "live a 'secular' life," to "share in God's sufferings"? Is that not the *cantus firmus* of the next century? Bonhoeffer made it clear that the religionless Christian "*may* live a 'secular' life (as one who has been *freed* from false religious obligations and inhibitions)" (LPP, 361, emphasis added). *Secular* and *religionlessness* are not identical. Secular — to exist secularly, in the world, in the *penultimate* — pertains to how one lives in the world. Religionlessness is the grace to deal with the world faithfully — dispensing with metaphysics, individualism, the deus ex machina, privilege, tutelage.

A secular Christian is, simply, a human being — a real person — not "a type of man" — African, European, Asian, and so forth — "but the [person] that Christ creates in us." If one has looked on *him,* one knows there is no hierarchy of races. And one finds beatitude in service to those who are suffering because of the illusion that there is. For it is deeply sinful to absolve oneself of the responsibility to suffer with them — so sinful that *only the suffering God can help.* This, I think, is what religionlessness means in a world grown up to the point of the twenty-first century. Without ducking his head in the sand of dogma, the religionless Christian will live in the real world, discovering its blessedness in the Other.

No religionless Christian acts as if we live in any other place but this world pulled apart by racist enmities. He or she has, therefore, a foot up on the world, understanding it better than it does itself — "namely on the basis of the Gospel and in the light of Christ" (LPP, 329). That surely means that one should recognize the analogy between the victims of racism and the image of God in the abused Christ. For God knows that we move toward the twenty-first century burdened by *that* suffering.

Ponder Africa. Is Bonhoeffer's legacy — "it is not the religious act that makes the Christian, but participation in the sufferings of God in the secular life" (LPP, 361) — *not* pertinent to the world of the beaten-down African Other? An African novelist captures the reality of it, as seen through the eyes of a Nigerian (Yoruba) spirit-child *(abiku)*. His name is Lazarus *(Azaro)*, and he sees

> a world of violence, of famine, of pullulating hunger, with beggars swarming the city center, with maggots devouring the inhabitants, with flies eating the eyeballs of children who were half-dead with starvation, with traffic jams everywhere, and people dying of hypertension at their steering wheels; with gases burning in the air, multiplying the ferocious heat of the sun; with housing projects built by corrupt businessmen collapsing and crushing to death their inhabitants all over the country; with soldiers going mad and shooting at people, emptying their guns at students, butchering their mothers, while riots quivered all over the landscapes; with the prisons overcrowded and exuding an unbearable stench of excrement and blood; with children poisoned by their mother's milk, the mother's having been poisoned by just about everything; with the rich and powerful gorging themselves at their bacchanalias, their feast of twenty-one slaughtered cows, their sweat reeking of vintage champagne, seven bands playing for their perfumed guests and weaving their patron's names in fulsome songs, while the food spilled on the polished floors and the guest trod

on them, while the choice delicacies changed into the writhing savory intestines of the dying children and women, who were gobbled up in celebrations without end. (Okri 1993, 89)

Okri does not exaggerate. What would kinship with those poor people mean?

According to Bonhoeffer, persons should share "in the suffering of God in Christ." Is not that, as Bonhoeffer put it, "metanoia: not in the first place thinking about one's own needs, problems, sins, and fears, but allowing oneself to be caught up into the way of Jesus Christ, into the messianic event, thus fulfilling Isa. 53" (LPP, 361-62). If we look on him and see that "he is despised and rejected of men; a man of sorrows, and acquainted with grief," would we not see others as well, and make common cause with *their* rejection?

Surely nothing so man-made and narrow as religion would get in the way of the discovery of a common humanity then. The faithful Christian will see: "Jesus calls [us] not to a new religion, but to life." *There's room for many a more.* The world will need such wholeness in the twenty-first century; must see that all that need matter is the exceedingly wide scope of grace — still costly because still bound to suffering.

How in keeping with Bonhoeffer's legacy it would be if wholeness were to entail the turn from the North, meaning the First World, to the South, meaning the Third World (with a focus on Africa). Ernst Feil suggests something similar to this: "Bonhoeffer no longer looked for help in the salvation of Occidental Christianity and Western culture" (Feil 1985, 199). Such Christianity had already had its day, and, as religions go, was waning. Even at its erudite best, it was, for Bonhoeffer, no more than *actus reflexus* — "a concept of intellectual history . . . a specifically Western phenomenon, and in that sense, 'a historically conditioned and transient form of human expression'" (197).

What is more, Bonhoeffer believed that Europe had succumbed to the void. He wrote: "It is in just this that it is western. It cannot break loose from its past. It cannot but be religious in essence" (E,

102). But, *faith* breaks from the past like a powerful locomotive: *I hear the car wheels rumbling, and rolling through the land/I hear the train a-coming, she's coming round the curve/She's loosened all her steam and brakes, and straining every nerve!* Nothing stops this train. It is incumbent upon Europe to get on board: Bonhoeffer "was confident that the church would continue to exist, but not because of the possibility of Europe experiencing a regeneration . . . rather, it was because God acts in the history of the world into which he entered through Jesus Christ" (Feil 1985, 199). His faith alone in the livingness of the power of this God-who-*acts*-and-*is* freed Bonhoeffer from sameness — from a religiosity so titanic as to deign to halt the gospel train.

"What Bonhoeffer knew about Europe and what he had learned in North America," writes Feil, moreover, "led him to be pessimistic about the future of the West. He shared the uncommon hope that new powers would radiate from Gandhi's India, which would be of value for Europe and North America as well, particularly in relation to Christian faith" (Feil 1985, 197). If one can believe Feil — Bonhoeffer's point that Asia had no historical heritage notwithstanding (E, 88) — Bonhoeffer's desire to study with Gandhi was no impetuous whim, but the foreshadowing of his interest in a religionless Christianity. If "religion is the Western form of Christianity" — if religionlessness means reveling in alterity — if "religionlessness is the form which, after the decline of the West, will take the place of religion as the dying form of Western Christian faith" — it would be fitting to look from the West to the Third World in the twenty-first century (Feil 1985, 196-97).

Anyone who has read Aloysius Pieris can appreciate this turn from the West and this focus on Asia. Pieris is from Sri Lanka — a context of such awesome indigence and of such significance for the problem of racism (given India's caste contradictions and own history of colonialism) that few should doubt the presence of Bonhoeffer's suffering God there. Pieris elucidates this in terms of Hinduism, but especially Buddhism, which enjoins the Christian to embrace the blessedness of voluntary poverty, as exemplified by the

Buddhist monks and the gospel witness to Christ. For Westerners to be so edified would surely be for them to be nonreligious in turning from sameness to otherness.

But remember the black Americans Bonhoeffer found so captivating. Remember the continent from which their ancestors were plundered. And in saying this I do not intend to leave out Latin America, or Europe's own impoverished masses. But when it comes to the problem of racism, when it comes to religionlessness that embraces what the West has considered as untouchable, Africa comes to the fore. African theologians — Engelbert Mveng, Jean-Marc Éla, Mercy Oduyoye, Kä Mana — certainly agree: Is there a better, perhaps the word is *worse,* place than Africa to appreciate why before God and with God, we live without God? Indeed, Kä Mana makes that point in his *Christ d'Afrique: Enjeux éthiques de la foi africaine en Jésus Christ:* What place moves one to leave religiousness *(système religieux)* behind more so than Africa? How will one respond to the challenges of religiouslessness *(champ non religieux)* if one does not respond to Africa? How will one see that Christ is not behind us, but before us if one is not moved to hope for freedom shoulder to shoulder with the African poor (Kä Mana 1994, 32)?

In any case, knowing what to do in the twenty-first century entails getting on board the gospel train where racism is forbidden — where we see Africans, Asians, Europeans, or whatever mixture of the three, to be sure, but especially the One who has been given us. And may we keep in mind, too, what Bonhoeffer wrote from prison — it is a wise thing to remember for the next hundred years:

> There remains an experience of incomparable value. We have learned for once to see the great events of world history from below, from the perspective of the outcast, the suspects, the maltreated, the powerless, the oppressed, the reviled — in short, from the perspective of those who suffer. The important thing is that neither bitterness nor envy should have gnawed at the heart during this time, that we should have come to look with new eyes

at matters great and small, sorrow and joy, strength and weakness, that our perception of generosity, humanity, justice and mercy should have become clearer, freer, less corruptible. We have to learn that personal suffering is a more effective key, a more rewarding principle for exploring the world in thought and action than personal good fortune. This perspective from below must not become the partisan expression of those who are eternally dissatisfied; rather, we must do justice to life in all its dimensions from a higher satisfaction, whose foundation is beyond any talk of "from below" or "from above." This is the way we may affirm it. (LPP, 17)

Yes — *so that our perception of generosity, humanity, justice and mercy* might *become clearer, freer, less corruptible.*

One can only thank Dietrich Bonhoeffer for sealing his witness with unimpeachable integrity. *I* surely thank him for letting his light shine in that way. For his witness — and the witnesses of several others, quick as well as dead — has convinced me that racism is as close to the reality of original sin as anything that threatens life today. Our holocausts prove that incontestably. I have the hope that those of us who suffer because this is so will find ways to resist this evil as nobly as Bonhoeffer did. Which is no veiled injunction to plot against racist tyrants. That was *Bonhoeffer's* call. This — *No Difference in the Fare* — is a call to freedom: *Get on board little children.*

Bibliography

Achebe, Chinua. 1989. *Hopes and Impediments.* Garden City, N.Y.: Anchor Books/Doubleday.

Adoukonou, Barthélemy. 1980. *Jalons pour une théologie africaine: Essai d'une herméneutique chrétienne du Vodun Dahoméen.* Vol. 1. Paris-Namur: Lethielleux.

Anderson, Jervis. 1983. *This Was Harlem: A Cultural Portrait, 1900-1950.* New York: Noonday Books/Farrar, Straus, Giroux.

Baldwin, James. 1981. *Go Tell It on the Mountain.* New York: Dell.

_____. 1995. "Sonny's Blues." In *Going to Meet the Man.* New York: Vintage/Random House.

Barth, Karl. 1967. *Church Dogmatics.* Vol. 4,2. Edinburgh: T & T Clark.

Bethge, Eberhard. 1985. *Dietrich Bonhoeffer: Man of Vision, Man of Courage.* Translated by Eric Mosbacher, Peter and Betty Ross, Frank Clarke, and William Glen-Doepel. New York: Harper & Row.

Bonhoeffer, Dietrich. 1954. *Life Together.* Translated by John Doberstein. New York: Harper & Row.

_____. 1959. *Creation and Fall* and *Temptation.* Translated by John C. Fletcher and Kathleen Downham. New York: Macmillan.

_____. 1961. *Act and Being*. Translated by Bernard Noble. New York: Harper and Brothers.

_____. 1963. *The Communion of Saints: A Dogmatic Inquiry into the Sociology of the Church*. Translated by R. Gregor Smith. New York: Harper & Row.

_____. 1963. *The Cost of Discipleship*. Rev. ed. Translated by R. H. Fuller. New York: Macmillan.

_____. 1977. "What Is a Christian Ethic." In *No Rusty Swords: Letters, Lectures and Notes from the Collected Works*. Vol. 1, edited by Edwin Robertson. Translated by John Bowden and Eberhard Bethge. London: Fontana Library/William Collins.

_____. 1977. "The First American Tour." In *No Rusty Swords. See above.*

_____. 1977. "Protestantism without Reformation." In *No Rusty Swords. See above.*

_____. 1977. "The Leader and the Individual in the Younger Generation." In *No Rusty Swords. See above.*

_____. 1977. "The Church and the Jewish Question." In *No Rusty Swords. See above.*

_____. 1977. "The Church and the Peoples of the World." In *No Rusty Swords. See above.*

_____. 1978. *Christ the Center*. Translated by Edwin Robertson. New York: Harper & Row.

_____. 1979. *Letters and Papers from Prison*. 2nd ed. Edited by Eberhard Bethge. New York: Macmillan.

_____. 1986. *Ethics*. Edited by Eberhard Bethge. Translated by Neville Horton Smith. New York: Macmillan.

Bosanquet, Mary. 1968. *The Life and Death of Dietrich Bonhoeffer*. New York: Harper & Row.

Carter, Guy, René van Eyden, Hans-Dirk van Hoogstraten, Jurjen Wiersma, eds. 1991. *Bonhoeffer's Ethics: Old Europe and New Frontiers*. Kampen: Kok Pharos.

Conrad, Joseph. 1970. *Heart of Darkness*. In *Eleven Modern Short Novels*. 2nd ed. Edited by Leo Hamalian and Edmond L. Volpe. New York: G. P. Putnam's Sons.

Courlander, Harold. 1993. *The African.* New York: Henry Holt.

Davidson, Basil. 1992. *The Black Man's Burden: Africa and the Curse of the Nation State.* New York: Times Books/Random House.

Day, Thomas. 1975. "Conviviality and Common Sense: The Meaning of Christian Community for Dietrich Bonhoeffer." Ph.D. diss., Union Theological Seminary.

de Gruchy, John. 1984. *Bonhoeffer and South Africa.* Grand Rapids: William B. Eerdmans.

Du Bois, W. E. B. 1969. *The Souls of Black Folk.* New York: New American Library.

_____. 1971. "History of the Negro Church: Africa to 1890." In *The Seventh Son.* Vol. 1. Edited by Julius Lester. New York: Random House.

Dumas, André. 1968. *Une théologie de la réalité: Dietrich Bonhoeffer.* Genève: Éditions labor et fides.

Eboussi-Boulaga, F. 1984. *Christianity without Fetishes.* Maryknoll, N.Y.: Orbis Books.

Ellison, Ralph. 1972. *Shadow and Act.* New York: Vintage Books/Random House.

Feil, Ernst. 1985. *The Theology of Dietrich Bonhoeffer.* Translated by Martin Rumscheidt. Philadelphia: Fortress Press.

Godsey, John. 1960. *The Theology of Dietrich Bonhoeffer.* Philadelphia: The Westminster Press.

Hamilton, Charles. 1992. *Adam Clayton Powell, Jr.* New York: Collier Books/Macmillan.

Hegel, Georg W. F. 1956. *The Philosophy of History.* Translated by J. Sibree. New York: Dover Publications.

Herskovits, Melville. 1967. *Dahomey: An Ancient West African Kingdom.* Vol. 1. Evanston: Northwestern University Press.

Hitler, Adolf. 1971. *Mein Kampf.* Translated by Ralph Manheim. Boston: Houghton Mifflin.

Hurston, Zora Neal. 1984. *Dust Tracks on a Road.* 2nd ed. Edited by Robert E. Hemenway. Chicago: University of Illinois Press.

Jefferson, Thomas. 1969. "On Negro Ability." In *Racial Thought in America: A Documentary History.* Vol. I: *From the Puritans to*

Abraham Lincoln. Edited by Louis Ruchames. Amherst: University of Massachusetts.

Johnson, James Weldon. 1990. *The Autobiography of an Ex-Colored Man.* Edited by William Andrews. New York: Penguin Books.

Jordan, Winthrop D. 1977. *White over Black: American Attitudes Toward the Negro, 1550-1812.* New York: W. W. Norton & Company.

Kä Mana. 1994. *Christ d'Afrique: Enjeux éthiques de la foi africaine en Jésus-Christ.* Paris: Karthala.

Kelly, Geffrey and F. Burton Nelson. 1990. *A Testament to Freedom: The Essential Writings of Dietrich Bonhoeffer.* San Francisco: Harper/Harper Collins.

Lovell, John. 1986. *Black Song: The Forge and the Flame.* New York: Paragon House.

Luther, Martin. 1972. *The Bondage of the Will.* In *Luther's Works.* Vol. 33, edited by Philip Watson. Philadelphia: Fortress Press.

Morrison, Toni. 1972. *The Bluest Eye.* New York: Washington Square Press.

_____. 1992. *Playing in the Dark: Whiteness and the Literary Imagination.* Cambridge: Harvard University Press.

Mudimbe, V. Y. 1988. *The Invention of Africa: Gnosis, Philosophy, and the Order of Knowledge.* Bloomington: Indiana University Press.

Okri, Ben. 1993. *Songs of Enchantment.* New York: Doubleday.

Ouloguem, Yambo. 1971. *Bound to Violence.* Translated by Ralph Manheim. Oxford: Heinemann.

Powell, Adam Clayton, Sr. 1938. *Against the Tide.* New York: Richard R. Smith.

Shipman, Pat. 1994. *The Evolution of Racism: Human Differences and the Use and Abuse of Science.* New York: Simon and Schuster.

Shirer, William. 1992. *The Rise and Fall of the Third Reich: A History of Nazi Germany.* New York: Fawcett Crest/Ballantine Books.

Stowe, Harriet Beecher. 1981. *Uncle Tom's Cabin.* New York: New American Library.

Thornton, John. 1992. *Africa and Africans in the Making of the Atlantic World, 1400-1680.* Cambridge: Cambridge University Press.

Ward, John W. 1981. Afterword to *Uncle Tom's Cabin* by Harriet Beecher Stowe. New York: Signet.

West, Cornel. 1982. *Prophesy Deliverance!* Philadelphia: Westminster Press.

Wood, Forrest. 1991. *The Arrogance of Faith: Christianity and Race in America from the Colonial Era to the Twentieth Century.* Boston: Northeastern University Press.

Wood, Peter. 1975. *Black Majority: Negroes in Colonial South Carolina from 1670 through the Stono Rebellion.* New York: W. W. Norton & Company.

Index of Names

Achebe, Chinua, 68, 93
Adoukonou, Barthélemy, 15, 17, 18, 97, 102-4, 106

Baldwin, James, 55
Barth, Karl, 42, 43, 71, 80
Bell, Bp. G. K. A., 43, 44
Bethge, Eberhard, 14, 22, 23, 30, 43, 48, 51, 57, 58, 154, 160, 164, 165
Bonhoeffer, Dietrich: association with Abyssinian Baptist Church, 42, 64, 65, 82, 83, 85, 114, 117; claim that "expulsion" of Jews is "expulsion of Christ," 148; desire to learn about India, 28, 33; desire to study with Gandhi, 28, 29, 34, 139, 169; disdain for an anti-Semite, 164; experience in Harlem, 26, 45, 51, 52, 58, 88, 89, 119, 123, 139; friendship with Frank Fisher, 13, 56, 57, 62, 89; identification with African-Americans, 26, 27, 64, 124, 170; influence of *Uncle Tom's Cabin* on, 90, 91; love of "Negro" spirituals, 21, 22, 45; on Africans sold into American slavery, 91, 92, 104; on "miscegenation," 153, 154; on "race" as ethical concept, 67, 68; on racism as heresy, 29; on racist division of American church, 123; on Scottsboro boys, 155; on the ridicule of "Negro dances," 154; on viewing history "from below," 170; opposition to Aryan clause, 29, 30, 32, 33, 52, 139; opposition to Hitler, 37, 38, 42-44, 132-34, 147, 150; refusal to exclude "Jewish-Christians" from the Church, 31, 137, 138; study of "Negro question" (race question), 26, 40, 117; study of African-American literature, 88, 115
Bonhoeffer, Julie (grandmother), 28
Bonhoeffer, Karl-Friedrich (brother), 26, 33
Bonhoeffer, Klaus (brother), 48
Bosanquet, Mary, 89

Calvin, John, 80

177

Conrad, Joseph, 93, 95
Courlander, Harold, 110
Cullen, Countee, 123

Davidson, Basil, 96
Day, Thomas, 23
de Gruchy, John, 13
Dohnanyi, Hans von, 42, 48
Du Bois, W. E. B., 88, 110, 112
Dumas, André, 14, 17, 19, 20, 22-24, 42

Ela, Jean-Marc, 170
Ellison, Ralph, 53, 116

Feil, Ernst, 15, 23, 65, 168, 169
Fisher, Frank, 13, 56, 57, 62, 89
Freud, Sigmund, 78

Gandhi, Mohandas K., 14, 23, 28, 29, 34, 35, 139, 169
Garvey, Marcus, 119, 120
Godsey, John, 14, 22, 23
Green, Clifford, 23

Haeckel, Ernst, 37
Hegel, Georg Wilhelm Friedrich, 77
Herskovits, Melville, 97, 106, 112
Hilderbrandt, Franz, 32, 131
Hitler, Adolf, 23, 31, 32, 34, 36-38, 42-44, 129-31, 147, 150, 152, 153, 155, 163, 164
Hughes, Langston, 25
Hume, David, 76
Hurston, Zora Neal, 109, 112

Jefferson, Thomas, 15, 16
Johnson, James Weldon, 115, 120
Jordan, Winthrop, 75

Kant, Immanuel, 53, 56, 76, 77

Lasserre, Jean, 34
Leibholz, Gerhard, 32, 131
Luther, Martin, 48, 80, 89, 109, 120-23, 128, 135, 137, 149

Mana, Ka, 170
Marle, Rene, 22
Mudimbe, V. Y., 15, 77
Muller, Hanfried, 22
Mveng, Engelbert, 170

Niebuhr, Reinhold, 39, 115
Niemoller, Martin, 30, 32, 42
Nietzsche, Friedrich, 148

Oduyoye, Mercy, 170
Okri, Ben, 168
Oster, Hans, 42
Ouologuem, Yambo, 108

Pieris, Aloysius, 169
Powell, Adam Clayton, Jr., 27, 115
Powell, Adam Clayton, Sr., 27, 88, 115-20

Rossler, Helmut, 122, 123

Shirer, William L., 30, 122
Stowe, Harriet Beecher, 90, 91, 93
Sutz, Erwin, 28, 33

Tagore, Rabindranath, 34
Tonnies, F., 63
Troeltsch, Ernst, 51

Visser 't Hooft, W. A., 43

Ward, John W., 91
West, Cornel, 76
Wood, Forrest, 22

Zwingli, U., 135